First World War
and Army of Occupation
War Diary
France, Belgium and Germany

1 INDIAN CAVALRY DIVISION
Headquarters, Branches and Services
Royal Army Service Corps
Assistant Director Supply and Transport
11 September 1914 - 30 September 1916

WO95/1169/4

The Naval & Military Press Ltd
www.nmarchive.com
Published in association with The National Archives

Published by

The Naval & Military Press Ltd

Unit 10 Ridgewood Industrial Park,

Uckfield, East Sussex,

TN22 5QE England

Tel: +44 (0) 1825 749494

www.naval-military-press.com

www.nmarchive.com

This diary has been reprinted in facsimile from the original. Any imperfections are inevitably reproduced and the quality may fall short of modern type and cartographic standards.

Contents

1 INDIAN CAV DIV

A D S & T

1914 SEP – 1916 SEP

WAR DIARY

of

A. D. S. & T., 1st Indian Cavalry Division.

From 11-9-14 To, 4-1-15.

Sheet 1.

Instructions regarding War Diaries and Intelligence Summaries are contained in F. S. Regs., Part II. and the Staff Manual respectively. Title pages will be prepared in manuscript.

WAR DIARY or ~~INTELLIGENCE~~ SUMMARY.

(*Erase heading not required.*)

of Lt Col. R. E. Vaughan, A D S + T 1st Indian Cavy Divn, Supply + Transport Corps

Army Form C. 2118.

Hour, Date, Place	Summary of Events and Information	Remarks and references to Appendices
Rawal Pindi, India 11th Septr 1914	Appointed A.D. Supplies, with Hd Qrs Cavy Divn proceeding on service overseas	Milly Secy to Cin C telegram 17301/9. Simla 11/9/14 –
Bombay 30 Octr 1914	Embarked mail steamer "Persia" P+O S N Coy	G.O.C. Rawal Pindi Divn telegram 1063 Camp 24-9-14 –
19th October 1914.	Disembarked Marseilles	
25 Oct. 1914.	Left Marseilles	
26 Octr 1914.	Arrived ~~ROUEN~~ ORLEANS. Reported to D.D.T. L of C Indian Contingent	
26 October to 30 Novr 1914	Remained in ~~Rouen~~ ORLEANS working in office of D.D.T. first engaged in formulating scheme for Advanced Transport Mule depot at ORLEANS and Base Transport Mule depot at MARSEILLES, the purpose of which was to ensure the regular replenishment of mule transport at the front. Then engaged in working out notes on the organisation + arrangements for the supply duties in the Indian Cavalry Division + obtaining information as to scales of rations, packing of supplies, + dealing with all matters relating	

Instructions regarding War Diaries and Intelligence Summaries are contained in F. S. Regs., Part II. and the Staff Manual respectively. Title pages will be prepared in manuscript.

WAR DIARY
or
~~INTELLIGENCE~~ SUMMARY.
(Erase heading not required.)

Lt Col R E Vaughan S.T. Corps

Army Form C. 2118.

Sheet 2.

Hour, Date, Place	Summary of Events and Information	Remarks and references to Appendices
ORLEANS 26 October to 30 Nov 1914.	to its equipment in transport, acting as assistant for this purpose to D.D.T. Saw loading of trains at advanced Base + A.S.C. system of despatches. Cavy Divn began to arrive at Marseilles on 7th Nov. and were quickly pushed up to ORLEANS. This caused a good deal of incon-venience at ORLEANS; D.D.T had asked that Division might not leave MARSEILLES till the Horse transport from England had been in ORLEANS for 2 days, to give time to fit up, as the ORLEANS Camps were far apart, + one a good way out, presenting difficulties of supply + water carriage when transport was short. Lt Col Moore D.S.O. S.T.C. had gone to England to fetch the Horse Transport. He brought over 91 G.S. Wagons, 24 Water Carts, 327 draught horses. He started with 368 horses but 40 were cast out at SOUTHAMPTON. Very shortly after arrival horses began to develop catarrh + fever + in a very	

(73989) W4141—463. 400,000. 9/14. H.&J.Ltd. Forms/C. 2118/10.

Instructions regarding War Diaries and Intelligence Summaries are contained in F. S. Regs., Part II. and the Staff Manual respectively. Title pages will be prepared in manuscript.

WAR DIARY of Lt Col R E Vaughan S.T.C.
or
~~INTELLIGENCE SUMMARY.~~
(*Erase heading not required.*)

Army Form C. 2118.
Sheet 3.

Hour, Date, Place	Summary of Events and Information	Remarks and references to Appendices
ORLEANS 25th to 30 Nov. 1914.	short time over 150 were sick. Eventually nearly all went sick & some died. Attempts were then made to fit up the Cavalry Division with other horses obtained by the Remount dept & sent to ORLEANS, and the wheeled field troop, the Umballa Cavalry Bde the Field Ambulance, Divnl Hd Qrs, Hd Qrs C.R.A., & Signal Squadron were equipped. But after the Umballa Bde had gone, it was discovered that horses being issued from Remount depot were showing temperatures & further issues were stopped, & transport horses with the Ambulance, Hd Qrs of Divn & CRA & signal squadron had to be exchanged just before embarkation in train for such seasoned horses as could be found from non-infected source & the deficit supplemented by pack mules. This put an end to equipping at ORLEANS & delayed the move of SIALKOT & LUCKNOW Bdes & whole of the RAA & headquarters, Divnl A.S.C. Eventually I.G.C. suggested sending all the wagons	

(73989) W4141—463. 400,000. 9/14. H.&J.Ltd. Forms/C. 2118/10.

Instructions regarding War Diaries and Intelligence Summaries are contained in F. S. Regs., Part II. and the Staff Manual respectively. Title pages will be prepared in manuscript.

WAR DIARY or ~~INTELLIGENCE SUMMARY~~. of Lt Col R E Vaughan S.T.C

(*Erase heading not required.*)

Army Form C. 2118.

Sheet 4

Hour, Date, Place	Summary of Events and Information	Remarks and references to Appendices
ORLEANS 26 Oct – 30 Nov 1914	and personnel to ROUEN to fit up & thence proceed to Railhead to meet the troops & equip them there. This was agreed to and after arranging trains the wagons & ambulances remaining (75 in all) & personnel (A.S.C. & Supervision from S.T.C.) left in two trains, the first under myself, the 2nd under Lt Col. Moore. [The latter had been appointed A.D.T. Cavy Divn. in India, but in FRANCE it was decided one A.D.S.&T. would suffice, & Col Moore was then used by D.D.T. L of C to go over & get the transport from England, pending appointment as A.D.S.&T. to a second Indian Cavy Divn mobilising in India & coming to FRANCE.] There were 41 vehicles & half the personnel on one train & 35 vehicles & rest of personnel on the other, & they started from ORLEANS on 30th Novr. 1914. During this stay at Orleans the detail & equipment of the supply personnel of the 1st Indian Cavy Division was worked out, & agreed to by D.D.S. Indian Contingent	

Instructions regarding War Diaries and Intelligence Summaries are contained in F. S. Regs., Part II. and the Staff Manual respectively. Title pages will be prepared in manuscript.

WAR DIARY
or
~~INTELLIGENCE~~ SUMMARY.

(*Erase heading not required.*)

Army Form C. 2118.

A/Lt Col R E Vaughan
S.T. Corps

Sheet 5

Hour, Date, Place	Summary of Events and Information	Remarks and references to Appendices
ORLEANS 26 October – 30 Nov 1914 –	agreed to the proposals in his No 85 dated 9 Nov 14. At the head quarters of Cavalry Divisional Supply & Transport Corps there were 1 officer, A.D.S.&T. (Lt Col R E Vaughan, I.A, S&T Corps) & 1 warrant officer (Cond^r J.A. Bosworth, S.T.C, Indian Departmental Unattached List) & one clerk, (Ambica Charan Bhose). Attached to this headquarters was the supply detail with the Divisional Troops; and a similar detail was attached to each Brigade H^d Qrs, for supply and requisitioning duties. Owing to shortage of officers it was not possible to give 2 officers with each of these units and the detail in each of the four formations consisted of 1 Officer S&T Corps 1 Warrant officer } S&T Corps, Indian Dept 2 Staff Sergeants } Unattached List 1 Indian Clerk 2 Indian agents, 10 Indian followers (3 Private & 3 public, viz 1 butcher & 4 weighmen)	

Sheet 6

Instructions regarding War Diaries and Intelligence Summaries are contained in F. S. Regs., Part II. and the Staff Manual respectively. Title pages will be prepared in manuscript.

WAR DIARY
or
INTELLIGENCE SUMMARY.
(Erase heading not required.)

Army Form C. 2118.

Hour, Date, Place	Summary of Events and Information	Remarks and references to Appendices
ORLEANS 26 Oct to 30 Nov 1914	1 horse – 1 pony – 1 motor car for requisitioning with driver, 3 bicycles for requisitioning up to 7. The detail was published in 1st Cavy Division orders, Pt II, No 12 of 21 Nov 1914. It seemed to be with difficulty that the personnel was produced, & in the case of agents it could not be completed and two tally clerks were utilised in place of two agents. In the same Divisional order was published the organisation of transport with the Division and the amount of transport allotted to all units	
30th Nov.	Left ORLEANS for ROUEN.	
1st Decr.	Arrived ROUEN & joined by Lt Col. Moore S.T.C. Proceeded to French barracks to take over horses. Found 221 horses ready. After some delay succeeded in getting arrangements made to have temperatures taken when large numbers were found with temperatures from 101° to 106°. The whole batch was	

(73989) W4141—463. 400,000. 9/14. H.&J.Ltd. Forms/C. 2118/10.

Sheet 7.

Instructions regarding War Diaries and Intelligence Summaries are contained in F. S. Regs., Part II. and the Staff Manual respectively. Title pages will be prepared in manuscript.

WAR DIARY
or
INTELLIGENCE SUMMARY.

(Erase heading not required.)

Army Form C. 2118.

Hour, Date, Place	Summary of Events and Information	Remarks and references to Appendices
ROUEN 1st to 5th Dec 1914	removed to sick lines. Another batch of 50 horses also came in, but these were healthy. The whole party of drivers, harness & remaining horses were moved up to the Remount depot, & there in the course of the next 3 days the necessary horses were provided. Brig Genl Moore D.V.S. came personally to investigate the circumstances.	
ROUEN 5th Dec	The party left ROUEN on 5th Dec & arrived BERGUETTE where they went into bivouac, & whence the transport was distributed to units as they arrived at BERGUETTE & LILLERS, the detail for LILLERS being taken over by a guide. On 10th Dec the detrainment was completed and the ~~[illegible]~~ supervising personnel rejoined their own formations. The weather was very bad for a great part of the time & the personnel suffered much, having to remain in the open to look after their horses.	

(73989) W4141—463. 400,000. 9/14. H.&J.Ltd. Forms/C. 2118/10.

Sheet 8

WAR DIARY or ~~INTELLIGENCE SUMMARY.~~

(*Erase heading not required.*)

Lt Col R E Vaughan
ADST 1st Ind Cavy Divn.

Army Form C. 2118.

Instructions regarding War Diaries and Intelligence Summaries are contained in F. S. Regs., Part II. and the Staff Manual respectively. Title pages will be prepared in manuscript.

Hour, Date, Place	Summary of Events and Information	Remarks and references to Appendices
LOZINGHEM 1.15 pm 20/12/14	orders for UMBALLA Bde to move, accompanied by UMBALLA Cavy Fd Ambulance + C Secn Divn Am Col. Rendezvous intimated by Bde Supply to ADST as GRANDE PLACE, BETHUNE. The supply column vehicles were in course of delivery + had to be checked in order to stand by and follow Bdes.	Railhead LILLERS Sheet 7. (from G.H.Q.)
	SIALKOT Bde also ordered to stand by with Am mn Col + Fd Ambce. Reported that this Bde had offloaded rations at usual hour 2.30 pm in its own Bde area, + in consequence, if a later order to move is received it cannot carry all its rations.	Am mn Railhead St VENANT. map France 1:80,000 Sheet 4 on BUERGETTE–MERVILLE Ry. Rev Lt Col
11.30 pm 20/12/14	SIALKOT Bde (less "Q" RHA) with SIALKOT Cavy Fd Ambce and SAA portion of Secn B. D.A.Col. ordered to move. A.Q.M.G. fixed Rendezvous at VENDIN-lez-Bethune 2.30 p.m. (just N. of main road between CHOCQUES + BETHUNE). He also wired UMBALLA fixing	map France 1:80,000 Sheet 7.
9. am 21/12/14	Rendezvous 21st at GRANDE PLACE, BETHUNE at 2.30 p.m. The Troops were called up to assist Indian Army Corps + came under orders of that Corps Commander. The LUCKNOW Bde were also ordered to stand ready.	RAILHEAD LILLERS (from G.H.Q.)
Rev Lt Col	Rendezvous of SIALKOT Bde subsequently advanced to BEUVRY about 2¼ miles to SE of BETHUNE. + orders wired to O.C. M.T. Supply Col. by A.Q.M.G.	map France Sheet 7 1:80,000

(73989) W4141—463. 400,000. 9/14. H.&J.Ltd. Forms/C. 2118/10.

13 Sheet 9.

Army Form C. 2118.

Instructions regarding War Diaries and Intelligence Summaries are contained in F. S. Regs., Part II. and the Staff Manual respectively. Title pages will be prepared in manuscript.

WAR DIARY
or
~~INTELLIGENCE SUMMARY.~~

of Lt Col. R.E. Vaughan A.D.S.T.

(*Erase heading not required.*)

Hour, Date, Place	Summary of Events and Information	Remarks and references to Appendices
LOZINGHEM 21-12-14	Loading of Supply Columns at Railhead has been done on a unit basis. The Division is scattered in billets about LILLERS, AUCHEL, BURBURE, ALLOUAGNE, all fairly close to railhead. Supply officers hand in each day to the Supply officer of the Divnl Supply Col. a detail of strength of units in their formation, with the quantities of supplies worked out. When the Supply train arrives at railhead it is seen if the supplies on the train are full or short. If short the difference is made up from a reserve kept up in the detail issue truck in which the Supply Officer, Railhead (a L of C. official & responsible to D.D.S.) so far as possible, but when the difference is considerable (as may be the case particularly with hay) the Supply officers of the Column have orders to average out the delivery so that all units may have an equal share. This means a considerable trouble in the revision of figures for loading tables which they have worked out the night before, & means that sometimes unloading is delayed. Railway trucks are loaded somewhat irregularly. The label on the outside of the truck rarely shews the correct contents, and the way bill & the contents of the train frequently fail to coincide. Thus when a supply officer sets out to work out	

(73989) W4141—463. 400,000. 9/14. H.&J.Ltd. Forms/C. 2118/10.

Instructions regarding War Diaries and Intelligence Summaries are contained in F. S. Regs., Part II. and the Staff Manual respectively. Title pages will be prepared in manuscript.

WAR DIARY
or
INTELLIGENCE SUMMARY.
(Erase heading not required.)

Army Form C. 2118.

Sheet 9

Hour, Date, Place	Summary of Events and Information	Remarks and references to Appendices
LOZINGHEM 21-12-14-	his loading tables for next loading he cannot be sure of results until trucks are empty, because both truck labels & way bills, (his only sources of information short of actual unloading) may differ from the actual load. The system of loading by units is convenient for delivery but is wasteful of lorry loading power. When small units are concerned they can best be grouped together in a lorry or lorries, which will be dealt with on receipt in one of two ways:- (a) It will dump its loads at a fixed point appointed by the Bde Supply officer, whence units would draw by the help of their horse transport (b) It would go round, as far as roads permit, to units billets, and issues be made from it in its capacity as a detail issue lorry. In the latter case care must be taken in packing the lorry so that all foods of the several kind may be easily accessible for issue from the truck. While the Division was stationary the former system tended to prevail because lorries had to go back to effect the delivery of hay, which was done by means of a second trip.	

Instructions regarding War Diaries and Intelligence Summaries are contained in F. S. Regs., Part II. and the Staff Manual respectively. Title pages will be prepared in manuscript.

WAR DIARY
or
~~INTELLIGENCE~~ SUMMARY.
(*Erase heading not required.*)

Lt Col R. E. Vaughan A.D.S.T.

Army Form C. 2118.

Sheet 9

Hour, Date, Place	Summary of Events and Information	Remarks and references to Appendices
LOZINGHEM 5.45 21-12-14, pm	Orders received for Ind. Cavy Corps to move quarters to new area - AIRE (excluded) ISBERGUES, St HILAIRE, AUCHY au bois, FEBVIN-PALFART, BONCOURT, ENQUIN, MAMETZ, all included -	Map FRANCE 1:80000 Sheet 4 + Sheet 7.
24-12-14	Division moved to new billets.	
25-12-14.	LUCKNOW Bde shifted further to west, + Divisional troops moved into NORRENT-FONTES. Hd Qrs established there.	
~~30-12~~ 4-Jany 15.	I made over charge (on transfer to Indian Cavy Corps Hd Qrs as AA + Q mg) of the 1st Ind: Cavy Dn to Lt Col C H G Moore D.S.O. S.T.C. on the afternoon of 4th Jany.	R E Vaughan Lt Col Indian Cavy S.T. Corps

WAR DIARY

of

A. D. of S. & T., 1st Indian Cavalry Division

From 5 - 1 - 1915 To 31 - 1 - 1915

	Look over duties of A D S + T 1st Indian Cavalry Division from Lt Col R.E. Vaughan S + T C	4/11/15 A.D. S + T. 1st. I. C. Dvn
5th " "	Visited Brigade areas	

(73989) W4141—463. 400,000. 9/14. H.&J.Ltd. Forms/C. 2118/10.

Instructions regarding War Diaries and Intelligence Summaries are contained in F. S. Regs., Part II. and the Staff Manual respectively. Title pages will be prepared in manuscript.

WAR DIARY
or
INTELLIGENCE SUMMARY.
(Erase heading not required.)

Army Form C. 2118.

Hour, Date, Place	Summary of Events and Information	Remarks and references to Appendices
6th January	Visited Brigade Areas	
7th January	Visited Brigade Areas.	
8th January	Routine work in office & went into question of fodder supply, visited rail head.	
9th " "	Routine work.	
10th " "	" "	
11th " "	Detailed Instructions received as to complement of MT vehicles now allotted to Supply Column & Ammunition Park vide No QV 119 of 11th January from DA & QMG Indian Cavalry Corps. The total result was reduction in Supply Column of 6 Workshop Lorries to 3 & increase in Ammt Park of 3 Three ton Lorries	
12th " "	Routine work.	
13th " "	Received orders to commence reconnaissance West of present billetting area with a view to	

(73989) W4141—463. 400,000. 9/14. H.&J.Ltd. Forms/C. 2118/10.

Army Form C. 2118.

Instructions regarding War Diaries and Intelligence Summaries are contained in F. S. Regs., Part II. and the Staff Manual respectively. Title pages will be prepared in manuscript.

WAR DIARY
or
INTELLIGENCE SUMMARY.
(*Erase heading not required.*)

Hour, Date, Place	Summary of Events and Information	Remarks and references to Appendices
	ascertaining resources of the Country in fodder.	
14th January	Selected Brigade Supply Officers of Lucknow & Amballa Brigades to undertake this work; no requisitioning officers having as yet been appointed to Brigades.	
15th "	Routine work.	
16th "	" "	
17th "	" "	
18th "	" "	
19th	Submitted report on resources of area. BOMY FRUGES, St OMER Rd west of DENNE BROEUCQ, ROUSSEAUVILLE and AMBRICOURT The result of the reconnaissance of this area was, that supplies of fodder were inadequate to allow of Division requisitioning its full requirements, all that could be	

(73989) W4141—463. 400,000. 9/14. H.&J.Ltd. Forms/C. 2118/10.

Instructions regarding War Diaries and Intelligence Summaries are contained in F. S. Regs., Part II. and the Staff Manual respectively. Title pages will be prepared in manuscript.

WAR DIARY
or
INTELLIGENCE SUMMARY.
(Erase heading not required.)

Army Form C. 2118.

Hour, Date, Place	Summary of Events and Information	Remarks and references to Appendices
	done, would be to supplement the two extra lbs fodder required to bring up the 10 lbs received from rail head, to the all round scale of 12 lbs.	
20th January	Detailed Capt BRUNKER Supply Officer Amballa Cavalry Brigade to carry out an extended Reconnaissance in area, MONTREUIL, ETAPLES, CRÉCY & RUE with a view to ascertaining the possibility of collecting supplies of fodder & utilising the line of railway from ETAPLES via MONTREUIL to ANVIN south of BERGUENEUSE to supply the Division with a full ration of fodder.	
21st " "	Visited BERGUENEUSE station with a view to utilising the light railway for carrying fodder. Ample room found for storage of fodder in the vicinity.	

Army Form C. 2118.

Instructions regarding War Diaries and Intelligence Summaries are contained in F. S. Regs., Part II. and the Staff Manual respectively. Title pages will be prepared in manuscript.

WAR DIARY
or
INTELLIGENCE SUMMARY.

(Erase heading not required.)

Hour, Date, Place	Summary of Events and Information	Remarks and references to Appendices
22nd	Called for reports from Brigades as to the possibility of procuring 4 lbs fodder per animal in their areas in lieu of 2 lbs, and made enquiries as to the possibility of using the light railway line from AIRE circling round to BERGUENEUSE to take out Rations to the Lucknow Brigade to enable Lorries thus freed to be utilised in bringing in loose fodder. The scheme was feasible. Trucks on light railway carry 10 tons, 2 trucks would be required.	
23rd	Visited ST HILAIRE to arrange a dumping place for rations in the event of a severe frost followed by a thaw, when Lorries will only be able to carry half loads over the remaining roads in area. Selected a place & communicated the same to the OC Divisional Supply column.	
24th	Went in to G.H.Q to see D.D.S	
25th	Issued instructions to Brigades re procedure	

(73989) W4141—463. 400,000. 9/14. H.&J.Ltd. Forms/C. 2118/10.

Army Form C. 2118.

Instructions regarding War Diaries and Intelligence Summaries are contained in F. S. Regs., Part II. and the Staff Manual respectively. Title pages will be prepared in manuscript.

WAR DIARY
or
INTELLIGENCE SUMMARY.
(*Erase heading not required.*)

Hour, Date, Place	Summary of Events and Information	Remarks and references to Appendices
	to be followed in the event of a Frost followed by a Thaw, vide 1st Indian Cavalry Divisional order No 3 of 25th January. The purport of the order was as follows. Fully laden Lorries will proceed as far as St HILAIRE drop half loads, leaving them in charge of the loaders of each Lorrie, the half loaded Lorries will proceed to destination, where units will have to provide six men each to do the off loading, which must be carried out with the greatest expedition to enable the Lorries to return & pick up loads.	
26th	Visited rail Hd in morning re question of shortage in fodder received & ordered. That the Amount Waybilled should be divided by the number of bales which arrived, this should give the average weight of bales, if still found that fodder short received, it would go to prove that	

(73989) W4141—463. 400,000. 9/14. H.&J.Ltd. Forms/C. 2118/10.

Instructions regarding War Diaries and Intelligence Summaries are contained in F. S. Regs., Part II. and the Staff Manual respectively. Title pages will be prepared in manuscript.

WAR DIARY
or
INTELLIGENCE SUMMARY.
(*Erase heading not required.*)

Army Form C. 2118.

Hour, Date, Place	Summary of Events and Information	Remarks and references to Appendices
	the amount waybilled was incorrect.	
	Visited G.H.Q & saw D.D.S & D of T re reorganisation of duties between Cavalry Corps & L of C.	
27th	Went in again to G.H.Q on above mentioned subject.	
28th	"	
29th	Visited Rail Head with a view to checking actual amounts of hay arriving from Base, as many complaints had been received of shortages in hay. The system followed has been to divide the total no of lbs waybilled by the number of bales arriving and if correct amount waybilled, the average thus arrived at for bales is a workable one, but it had been found that the bales were short weight, I had every bale checked by its detailed weight & found the total weight was some 8,000 lbs short of what had been waybilled. I reported to D.D.S G.H.Q & he has wired Base & informed D.G.S. 10.30pm received orders for Division to stand ready to move at 2 hours notice.	

Instructions regarding War Diaries and Intelligence Summaries are contained in F. S. Regs., Part II. and the Staff Manual respectively. Title pages will be prepared in manuscript.

WAR DIARY
or
INTELLIGENCE SUMMARY.
(*Erase heading not required.*)

Army Form C. 2118.

Hour, Date, Place	Summary of Events and Information	Remarks and references to Appendices
30th January	Orders received for U D & A Batteries with Artillery Sections Ammunition Column & Park to be detached to 5th Corps temporarily. The Batteries & Ammn Column & Park moved on 30th to Billets at FONTES, BOESEGHEM and STEENBECQUE. The Supply Column was ordered to divert the necessary number of Lorries to ration them at above named places & this was done.	
31st January	5th Corps asked for 9.30cwt Lorries to be allotted to 28th Division Supply Column to serve Batteries at detached on 30th. OC Divisional Supply Column 1st Indian Cavalry Division was ordered to comply. The Lorries to fill up at AIRE railhead, proceed to HAZEBROUCK & report to OC D S Column 28th Division for orders and from this date to come under orders of OC D S Column 28th Division.	

C H Moore Lt. Col.
A. D. Sst. 1st I. C. Div.
31-1-15.

(73989) W4141—463. 400,000. 9/14. H.&J.Ltd. Forms/C. 2118/10.

Instructions regarding War Diaries and Intelligence Summaries are contained in F. S. Regs., Part II. and the Staff Manual respectively. Title pages will be prepared in manuscript.

WAR DIARY
or
INTELLIGENCE SUMMARY

(Erase heading not required.)

Army Form C. 2118.

Hour, Date, Place	Summary of Events and Information	Remarks and references to Appendices
1st February.	Took over appointment of OC ASC. 1st Indian Cavalry Division from Lt Col Moore S&T Corps. Visited all Supply Officers in Divl Area and inspected Supply Diaries. Recd intimation that owing to thaw barriers would be put up on certain roads and arranged with O/c S Coln to carry full load as far as ST HILAIRE dump loads and make two trips. Referred question whether it is at all necessary to ½ load 30 cwt lorries. Possibly the double trip with ½ loads does more harm to the roads than the single trip with full loads.	
2nd February.	Called for reports from Supply Officers as to the method of purchasing and issued orders that prices paid [illegible] be entered in weekly purchase statements. As no statement showing strength of [illegible] was in office instructed S.O's to submit weekly instead of only Brigade totals.	

Instructions regarding War Diaries and Intelligence Summaries are contained in F. S. Regs., Part II. and the Staff Manual respectively. Title pages will be prepared in manuscript.

WAR DIARY
or
INTELLIGENCE SUMMARY

(Erase heading not required.)

Army Form C. 2118.

Hour, Date, Place	Summary of Events and Information	Remarks and references to Appendices
	Went to see A.A. & Q.M.G. Indian Cavalry Corps on subject of relative duties of O.C. A.S.C. and Senior Supply Officer as Provisional instructions issued appeared to leave out the O.C. A.S.C.	
	Major Norman Young S&T Corps reported his arrival as Senior Supply Officer.	
	Decided by G.O.C. no guards were to be left over excess Rt. & ch. of Div. moved but that they were to be taken up and left in charge of the Maire.	
3rd February.	Visited Railhead and saw lorries being loaded. Received reports from Supply officers on system of purchasing supplies and sent notes on same to A.A. & Q.M.G. Indian Cavalry Corps.	
	Received orders for ½ loaded lorries ½ loaded G.S. Wagons A.T. Carts full loads.	
4th February.	Accompanied Supply Column lorries and saw distribution to Units.	
	Inspected Horse and Mule transport of Amballa Brigade found the transport in a good state.	

1247 W 3299 200,000 (E) 8/14 J.B.C. & A. Forms/C. 2118/11.

Instructions regarding War Diaries and Intelligence Summaries are contained in F. S. Regs., Part II. and the Staff Manual respectively. Title pages will be prepared in manuscript.

WAR DIARY
or
INTELLIGENCE SUMMARY
(Erase heading not required.)

Army Form C. 2118.

Hour, Date, Place	Summary of Events and Information	Remarks and references to Appendices
	except that wool, rewar and serge for mule saddles was urgently required. Necessary indents had been submitted and I have taken necessary steps to expedite supply.	
5th February	Inspected A.T. Carts (Bhurtpore - Imperial Service Transport) of Divisional Amn Column. These are steel carts except for the wheels. The carts generally are in a bad state - no spare parts - no artificers and must have been sent in a most unsatisfactory state as axle arms, pipe boxes show excessive wear which could not have occurred since arrival in France. Some of the axles are bent throwing the wheels as much as 8 inches out of line. I understand it is intended to change these carts for G.S. wagons and the sooner it is done the better. The ordinary A.T. cart is excellent and will stand very rough usage but the carts in question are difficult to repair and have never been looked.	

Instructions regarding War Diaries and Intelligence Summaries are contained in F. S. Regs., Part II. and the Staff Manual respectively. Title pages will be prepared in manuscript.

WAR DIARY
or
INTELLIGENCE SUMMARY

(Erase heading not required.)

Army Form C. 2118.

Hour, Date, Place	Summary of Events and Information	Remarks and references to Appendices
	after.	
	In the afternoon attended inspection of Divl Supply Column by Indian Cavalry Corps commander.	
	Orders for ½ loads on lorries and G S wagons withdrawn	
	Inspected transport of Divl Hd Qrs Sialkote and Ambala Field Ambulances – everything very satisfactory.	
6th February.	With Senior Supply Officer interviewed AA & QMG. on subject of duties of OC ASC. and Senior Supply Officer when the Division is moving – Arranged that while halted the Supply Column and all Supply Officers shd be practised in actual duties on the march twice a week as far as present conditions admit – Rendezvous will be given – Supply Officers will meet S.S.O. orders for the 2nd Rendezvous will be issued and various necessary reports made –	

1247 W 3299 200,000 (E) 8/14 J.B.C. & A. Forms/C. 2118/11.

Instructions regarding War Diaries and Intelligence Summaries are contained in F. S. Regs., Part II. and the Staff Manual respectively. Title pages will be prepared in manuscript.

WAR DIARY
or
INTELLIGENCE SUMMARY.
(*Erase heading not required.*)

Army Form C. 2118.

Hour, Date, Place	Summary of Events and Information	Remarks and references to Appendices
	I inspected transport of Field Troop. Lucknow Field Ambulance and No 4 Divl Engineers. The first two were in good ~~condition~~ condition - the last wanted a good deal of attention	
	It was brought to notice that Drivers of Lorries very often kept engines running slowly while halted for off loading supplies. Orders issued to prevent waste of petrol.	
7th February.	In consultation with senior supply officer and O/c Divl Supply Column went into detail of System of Supply and duties of all officers concerned. Drafted orders for the approval of A.A. & QMG	
8th February.	Visited Rail Head.	
9th "	Arranged with AA & QMG for practise of Lucknow system of supply. All ~~officers~~ supply officers to be at 1st Rendezvous & necessary orders issued as if Divn was marching.	

Instructions regarding War Diaries and Intelligence Summaries are contained in F. S. Regs., Part II. and the Staff Manual respectively. Title pages will be prepared in manuscript.

WAR DIARY
or
INTELLIGENCE SUMMARY.
(Erase heading not required.)

Army Form C. 2118.

Hour, Date, Place	Summary of Events and Information	Remarks and references to Appendices
10th February	Went out with Divl. Supply Column & followed supply system to Units. Supply Officers joined at First Rendezvous & necessary orders were issued up to time Supply Column left for Railhead	
11th February	Inspected 1st Line Transport of Sialkote Brigade	[illegible]
	<u>Horses</u> in very good condition with exception of 3	
	<u>Mules</u> in very fair condition but many feet too long	
	<u>Harness</u> in fair order. Dubbin required. Some panels require replacement. Serge & wool required for repairs	
	<u>Wagons</u> in good order except that "tires" are wanting on nearly all	
	<u>A.T. Carts</u> Good carts generally serviceable. Split pins required for pole wheels; drag washers wanting in some cases.	

(73989) W4141—463. 400,000. 9/14. H.&J.Ltd. Forms/C. 2118/10.

Instructions regarding War Diaries and Intelligence Summaries are contained in F. S. Regs., Part II. and the Staff Manual respectively. Title pages will be prepared in manuscript.

WAR DIARY
or
INTELLIGENCE SUMMARY.
(*Erase heading not required.*)

Army Form C. 2118.

Hour, Date, Place	Summary of Events and Information	Remarks and references to Appendices
	The [illegible] carts are not in good order. Action taken but there is great delay in obtaining repairing material & spare parts from Ordnance Dept.	H
12th February.	Inspected transport of Signal ~~[illegible]~~ Squadron. Inspected in the afternoon transport of LUCKNOW Brigade. Generally the transport requires better supervision. A.T. Carts want general tightening up, tail boards of most of the G.S. Wagons are broken due to bad driving & not keeping distance. Issued instructions to Brigades on all points which require attention.	
13th February	Present at inspection of Divl. Commander of Tongas of Signal Troops. Some of these tongas are quite unsuitable, being weak in construction & all of them have the drawback of different specifications so that replacing broken or worn parts wd. be most difficult.	

(73989) W4141—463. 400,000. 9/14. H.&J.Ltd. Forms/C. 2118/10.

Instructions regarding War Diaries and Intelligence Summaries are contained in F. S. Regs., Part II. and the Staff Manual respectively. Title pages will be prepared in manuscript.

WAR DIARY
or
INTELLIGENCE SUMMARY
(Erase heading not required.)

Army Form C. 2118.

Hour, Date, Place	Summary of Events and Information	Remarks and references to Appendices
	An AT Cart owing to it's having no tail boards & spaces through which small articles might fall through, is unsuitable. I am making a suitable arrangement to allow of packing the load securely.	
14th February	Went through a scheme with AA & QMG, for a staff ride (Supply).	[illegible]
15th "	Went out with AA & QMG. accompanied Div^t Supply Column & followed supply system to Units. Supply Officers joined at First Rendezvous & necessary orders were issued up to time Supply Column left for Railhead	[illegible]
16th "	Office routine.	[illegible]
17th "	" "	
18th	" " "	
19th "	Proceeded with AD of S Cavalry Corps to LUCKNOW Brigade with reference to supply of fodder in vicinity	

1247 W 3299 200,000 (E) 8/14 J.B.C. & A. Forms/C. 2118/11.

Instructions regarding War Diaries and Intelligence Summaries are contained in F. S. Regs., Part II. and the Staff Manual respectively. Title pages will be prepared in manuscript.

WAR DIARY
or
INTELLIGENCE SUMMARY
(Erase heading not required.)

Army Form C. 2118.

Hour, Date, Place	Summary of Events and Information	Remarks and references to Appendices
20th February	Administrative Staff ride. Officers attending AA & QMG, DA & QMG, O/C. ASC, Adjutant, all Supply Officers, Staff Captains, O/C. Divl Supply Column + 2 Section Officers. Divl S. Col was represented by 6 lorries Two systems were tried (1) Supply Officers joining the S. Col at 1st Rendezvous (2) Supply Officers obtaining orders from Brigade Staff as to Final Rendezvous + billetting areas + having reconnoitred roads proceeding to Final Rendezvous. The results will be discussed tomorrow	
21st February	The conclusions arrived at regarding yesterdays Administrative Staff ride included the view that the most convenient place for Brigade Supply Officers was with their respective Bdes until they had reconnoitred the roads between units + some central point which would be the Bde Rendezvous – Thence they would go to the Final Rendezvous and bring up the Bde Section of the Dl Supply Column. This system is to be carried out next staff ride.]	

1247 W 3299 200,000 (E) 8/14 J.B.C. & A. Forms/C. 2118/11.

Instructions regarding War Diaries and Intelligence Summaries are contained in F. S. Regs., Part II. and the Staff Manual respectively. Title pages will be prepared in manuscript.

WAR DIARY
or
INTELLIGENCE SUMMARY

(Erase heading not required.)

Army Form C. 2118.

Hour, Date, Place	Summary of Events and Information	Remarks and references to Appendices
22nd February.	Carcases slaughtered by Hindus are to be kept apart from those killed by Mohdns by enclosing the former in a clean cornsack. Some Hindus have rejected their meat owing to it having touched other sects carcases.	
23rd February.	Arrangements made for lifting men towards the front in the DSC lorries tomorrow & for a few days to come. It is notable that the 30 cwt lorry carries 20 men & require 10% spare lorries.	
24th February	Routine duties – The move of troops in lorries went off very well. No deficiencies at Railhead. Saw A/C Bhurtpore carts pass today. Very awful carts – they are military obstacles very like wire entanglements. They are or will be surplus when we get the promised G.S. wagons.	
25th February.	Busses replaced lorries for conveying digging parties. Bus unit War Estab not laid down or known so that when ordered to issue rations to "28 buses" it was not clear what the ration strength was. Nor was it easy to "provide petrol" without any data as to their mileage per gallon – In the end they turned up with rations & ample petrol. so our preparations tho' complete were not required. Saw the Bhurtpore Iron Transport carts today. They are being seen to but are very nearly worn out as regards carts.	

1247 W 3299 200,000 (E) 8/14 J.B.C. & A. Forms/C. 2118/11.

Instructions regarding War Diaries and Intelligence Summaries are contained in F. S. Regs., Part II. and the Staff Manual respectively. Title pages will be prepared in manuscript.

WAR DIARY
or
INTELLIGENCE SUMMARY

(Erase heading not required.)

Army Form C. 2118.

Hour, Date, Place	Summary of Events and Information	Remarks and references to Appendices
26th February	The preference of Indian Troops for potatoes & fresh vegetables for fruits preserved was communicated to DDS&T. – Some 'Lumber mens socks' were doled out for trial – quality looks good & of the samples (10 prs) the wool seemed pure & the main peculiarities were their warmth & the peculiar heel (worked on a radial pattern, the heel being a quadrant). 2 days given in which to form & gather opinions –	
27th February.	Question arose today in one Bde as to whether a Mule driver is justified in refusing to tie on the loading ropes & to load up. Of course he is not. – I pointed out that it is inexpedient & directly opposed to Army practice to attempt to make drivers load up. Troops must do it. Went to St Venant to see the Bus unit gets fed & got at their organization in case they are attached to us again suddenly for rations.	
28th Feby.	Nothing noteworthy today – Buses now furnished with about 100 lbs straw each to keep diggers wet feet from giving them ill effects – a sound precaution & one which is easily taken & may save several casualties.	

Instructions regarding War Diaries and Intelligence Summaries are contained in F. S. Regs., Part II. and the Staff Manual respectively. Title pages will be prepared in manuscript.

WAR DIARY
or
INTELLIGENCE SUMMARY
(Erase heading not required.)

Army Form C. 2118.

Hour, Date, Place	Summary of Events and Information	Remarks and references to Appendices
1st March	O/C Div^l Supply Column applied for three additional motor bicycles as being essential for keeping up communication with Supply Column & also to have spares in case of a breakdown. The 9 motor bicycles at present allotted to the Column are worked to their full capacity	
2nd March	Reference to letter from Cavalry Corps that some means sh^d be adopted for warning drivers of faster moving vehicles coming up from behind. Suggested by Cavalry Corps that a string sh^d be tied to drivers arm & manipulated by those men riding in rear of lorry. This suggestion is considered dangerous as it might affect the drivers steering & an experiment is being made with a bell in cab manipulated by those men riding in rear of lorry & also	

1247 W 3299 200,000 (E) 8/14 J.B.C. & A. Forms/C. 2118/11.

Instructions regarding War Diaries and Intelligence Summaries are contained in F. S. Regs., Part II. and the Staff Manual respectively. Title pages will be prepared in manuscript.

WAR DIARY
or
INTELLIGENCE SUMMARY
(Erase heading not required.)

Army Form C. 2118.

Hour, Date, Place	Summary of Events and Information	Remarks and references to Appendices
	by using a special trigger which can be used by Brook man.	
3rd March.	The three Batteries of R.H.A. marched to join the 8th Division. Detailed Capt. Bell-Murray to proceed as T.O. with a Sergt & 1 corpl for Supply duties. Eleven G.S. Wagons withdrawn from Field Squadron to be used for Supply while the Batteries are attached to the 8th Division.	
4th March	Inspected Transport of Lucknow Brigade & found a very great improvement. Harness, vehicles etc all in excellent state.	
5th March	Office routine.	
7th "	As Cook's wagons are now in "A" Echelon issued orders that they sh^d be horsed with "light draught horses"	
8th "	The three Brigades were ordered to concentrate &	

1247 W 3299 200,000 (E) 8/14 J.B.C. & A. Forms/C. 2118/11.

WAR DIARY
or
INTELLIGENCE SUMMARY
(Erase heading not required.)

Army Form C. 2118.

Instructions regarding War Diaries and Intelligence Summaries are contained in F. S. Regs., Part II. and the Staff Manual respectively. Title pages will be prepared in manuscript.

Hour, Date, Place	Summary of Events and Information	Remarks and references to Appendices
	at night occupied the following billetting areas. UMBALLA Bde LIGNY & FLECHIN. LUCKNOW Bde FEBVIN – FONTAINE – LIVOSSART. SIALKOTE Bde LIERES – AUCHY – WESTERHEM. Div! Troops as before. The whole procedure as regards Supply Column was carried out. Lorries not off loaded till orders were given, reports that troops had been fed received etc. Everything worked smoothly.	
9th March.	Office routine.	
10th "		
11th "	Division moved to vicinity of MARLES & occupied the BOIS DES DAMES. Sialkote [illegible] marched independently. Ditto Div! Troops. Transport of LUCKNOW & UMBALLA Brigades, starting Pt NEDONCELLE 6.35 AM. The transport marched via PERNES to MARLE. Various points as regards "March Discipline" were brought to light & instructions have been issued to all T.O's	

1247 W 3299 200,000 (E) 8/14 J.B.C. & A. Forms/C. 2118/11.

Instructions regarding War Diaries and Intelligence Summaries are contained in F. S. Regs., Part II. and the Staff Manual respectively. Title pages will be prepared in manuscript.

WAR DIARY
or
INTELLIGENCE SUMMARY
(Erase heading not required.)

Army Form C. 2118.

Hour, Date, Place	Summary of Events and Information	Remarks and references to Appendices
12th March	Division moved into billets on night of 11th as follows Hd Qrs Divn & SIALKOTE Bde – MARLE. LUCKNOW Bde – AUCHEL. UMBALLA Bde – FLORINGHEM & CAUCHY. SAA Divl Ammn Column & LUCKNOW Fd Amb: – AUCHEL	
13th "	Final Rendezvous – RAMBERT.	
13th "	Final Rendezvous – RAMBERT	
14th "	Recd orders in the evening that Division will move during the night to following Billetting Areas Div. Hd Qrs, Field Ambulances & Signal Squadron – BOURECQ. Field Troop – LES PESSES. Ammunition Column – WESTREHEM. Sialkote Bde – ST HILAIRE – COTTES – LIERES. Lucknow Bde [illegible] – FLECHIN – BONCOURT – PIPPEMONT & FEBVIN. Umballa Bde FONTAINE LES HERMANS – NEDONCHELLE – NEDON AMETTES. Saw transport of Brigades marched independently. Went to Starting Pt & [illegible] at CAUCHY & saw the transport pass between 10 pm & midnight. Road discipline on the whole good. Supplies were not issued.	

1247 W 3299 200,000 (E) 8/14 J.B.C. & A. Forms/C. 2118/11.

Instructions regarding War Diaries and Intelligence Summaries are contained in F. S. Regs., Part II. and the Staff Manual respectively. Title pages will be prepared in manuscript.

WAR DIARY
or
INTELLIGENCE SUMMARY

(Erase heading not required.)

Army Form C. 2118.

Hour, Date, Place	Summary of Events and Information	Remarks and references to Appendices
15th March	Supply Column brought up supplies in the early morning for 15th & again in the afternoon for 16th	
16th "	Office routine	
17th "	"	
18th "	Billetting areas as follows:—	
	Divl Hd Qrs } Signal Squadron } ENQUIN	
	Hd Qrs ASC BERNY.	
	Field Squadron ERNY	
	Ammtn Column WESTREHEM	
	Ammn Park "	
	Field Ambulances RELY.	
	SIALKOT Bde.	
	Hd Qrs AMES	
	6th Cavly "	
	19th Lancers BELLERY.	
	17th " LIERES	

1247 W 3299 200,000 (E) 8/14 J.B.C. & A. Forms/C. 2118/11.

Instructions regarding War Diaries and Intelligence Summaries are contained in F. S. Regs., Part II. and the Staff Manual respectively. Title pages will be prepared in manuscript.

WAR DIARY
or
INTELLIGENCE SUMMARY

(Erase heading not required.)

Army Form C. 2118.

Hour, Date, Place	Summary of Events and Information	Remarks and references to Appendices
	AMBALA Bde	
	Hd Qrs — AMETTES	
	30th Lancers — "	
	9th Hodson's Horse — NEDON	
	8th Hussars — NEDONCHELLE, FONTAINE-LES-HERMANS	
	LUCKNOW Bde	
	Hd Qrs — LIETTRES Chateau	
	36th Jacob's Horse — LINGHEM, LIETTRES	
	29th Lancers — ESTREE BLANCHE, FLECHINELLE	
	K.D.G.'s — FLECHINELLE, BONCOURT, CUHEM	
11th March	Inspected 36 carts of Divl Ammn Col. At present there some carts of 31st Mule Corps with Divl Ammn Col & some carts of Bhurtpore Imperial Transport with Brigades. Am arranging to transfer all the latter to Divl Ammn Column so that Bhurtpore carts may be together under their Comdg Officer	

Instructions regarding War Diaries and Intelligence Summaries are contained in F. S. Regs., Part II. and the Staff Manual respectively. Title pages will be prepared in manuscript.

WAR DIARY
or
INTELLIGENCE SUMMARY
(Erase heading not required.)

Army Form C. 2118.

Hour, Date, Place	Summary of Events and Information	Remarks and references to Appendices
21st March	Inspected 36 carts of Divl. Ammtn Col. Great improvement in the case of carts which are in a fairly good state with exception of some very old pattern wheels. The following Officers Indian Army Reserve joined as Regimental transport Officers: Lt H.W. HURST – SIALKOTE Bde. Lt H CRAWFORD – Ambala Bde. Lt A. RICHARDS – Lucknow Bde.	
22nd March	Inspected transport of LUCKNOW Fd Ambulance.	
23rd "	Recd orders for 2 W.O's to be returned to Base & 1 Sergt. to be transferred to LUCKNOW Fd Amb: this was consequent on arrival of Regimental transport Officers. Conductors TURNER & Sub Conductor COSTELLO to Base & Sergt MURRAY to Fd Ambulance. Recd orders re arrival of Horse transport for 2 Battns Connaught Rangers in relief of mule transport also a detail of mule transport to be ready to be despatched to MARSEILLES.	

1247 W 3299 200,000 (E) 8/14 J.B.C. & A. Forms/C. 2118/11.

Army Form C. 2118.

WAR DIARY
or
INTELLIGENCE SUMMARY
(Erase heading not required.)

Instructions regarding War Diaries and Intelligence Summaries are contained in F. S. Regs., Part II. and the Staff Manual respectively. Title pages will be prepared in manuscript.

Hour, Date, Place	Summary of Events and Information	Remarks and references to Appendices
24th March.	Went to WESTREHEM to arrange with Major Watson BHURTPORE Imperial Service Transport re despatch of transport & establishment	
25th "	Ditto	
26th "	Inspected transport of Ambala Bde & Fd Ambulance. In good condition generally but many faults not yet rectified — washers wanting on AT Carts & many tailboards broken in G.S. Wagons. Reported to AA & QMG with suggestions for action. Indian Cav'y Regts do not take sufficient interest in their transport.	
27th "	Rode to AIRE to see A.D.S. & T. re despatch of mule transport. Informed ADST transport wd be ready 29th	
28th "	Suggested to AA & QMG that Regts sd drill the A.S.C. drivers & generally smarten them up.	

Army Form C. 2118.

Instructions regarding War Diaries and Intelligence Summaries are contained in F. S. Regs., Part II. and the Staff Manual respectively. Title pages will be prepared in manuscript.

WAR DIARY
or
INTELLIGENCE SUMMARY

(Erase heading not required.)

Hour, Date, Place	Summary of Events and Information	Remarks and references to Appendices
29th March	Inspected transport of SIALKOTE Bde. All in very good order except tailboards of G.S. Wagons 19th Lancers.	
	Inspected 106 AT Carts BHURTPORE Transport at BERGUETTE. Orders to entrain at 10.30 AM tomorrow	
30th "	Visited Railhead	
31st "	Arranged details of Departmental Staff Ride with AA&QMG to be held on 3rd April to practise S & T. officers in supply duties on the march & the marching of B. Echelon transport	
	H. Arrington Lt Colonel O/C. A.S.C. 1st Indn Cav. Div.	

1247 W 3299 200,000 (E) 8/14 J.B.C. & A. Forms/C. 2118/11.

Instructions regarding War Diaries and Intelligence Summaries are contained in F. S. Regs., Part II. and the Staff Manual respectively. Title pages will be prepared in manuscript.

WAR DIARY
or
INTELLIGENCE SUMMARY

(Erase heading not required.)

Army Form C. 2118.

Hour, Date, Place	Summary of Events and Information	Remarks and references to Appendices
1st April	Went to see ADS&T re withdrawal of AT Carts for carrying horse rugs (8 per Regt, 2 per Battery + 2 Divl Hd Qrs total 80). As the Batteries are attached to an Infy Divn it was decided to leave the rug carts with the Batteries & withdraw 74 carts from the Division. These carts to be ready for entrainment on 7th April. Issued necessary orders for carts to be collected at Divl Hd Qrs on 5th	
2nd April	Inspected the transport of Field Ambulances. The two tanks for water (Indians) are carried on Indian vehicles which require to be exchanged for stronger carts. Action taken to report the matter.	
3rd "	Collected 74 AT Carts [illegible] [illegible] + [illegible] ready for despatch (Rug carts) by rail	
4th "	Ordered despatch of rug carts to BERGUETTE	

1247 W 3299 200,000 (E) 8/14 J.B.C. & A. Forms/C. 2118/11.

Instructions regarding War Diaries and Intelligence Summaries are contained in F. S. Regs., Part II. and the Staff Manual respectively. Title pages will be prepared in manuscript.

WAR DIARY
or
INTELLIGENCE SUMMARY

(Erase heading not required.)

Army Form C. 2118.

Hour, Date, Place	Summary of Events and Information	Remarks and references to Appendices
	The four A.S. Corps Officers appointed as Brigade T.O.s are too junior for the appointment. they have only a few months service & are all junior to the Regtl. C.O.s also they cannot converse with Indians. I suggested that these officers might be exchanged for S & T. Corps officers from the LAHORE & MEERUT Divisional Trains where many senior officers were doing subaltern's work. Interviewed O/C. LAHORE Divl. Train who agreed to let some of his officers go & the question is now being gone into.	
5th April	Office routine	
6th	Inspected the transport of LUCKNOW Bde & accompanied it for some distance on the march to test "March Discipline". Very satisfactory but in some cases "sections" were not drawn & teams & some AT. Carts were too long	
	Received information that AT carts at starting be	

1247 W 3299 200,000 (E) 8/14 J.B.C. & A. Forms/C. 2118/11.

Instructions regarding War Diaries and Intelligence Summaries are contained in F. S. Regs., Part II. and the Staff Manual respectively. Title pages will be prepared in manuscript.

WAR DIARY
or
INTELLIGENCE SUMMARY
(Erase heading not required.)

Army Form C. 2118.

Hour, Date, Place	Summary of Events and Information	Remarks and references to Appendices
	replaced by 4 horsed vehicles to be driven by men drawn from Regiments — arrangements are being made to train these men now.	
	The 20 AT Pack mules will be replaced by 22 Ordnance mules.	
7th April	Submitted indent for two G.S. Wagons to replace two civilian wagons	
8th "	Office routine	
9th "	I. Cavalry Corps asked for information as to how many lorries in Div. S. Column were capable of carrying 35 cwt to 2 Tons [illegible]	
10th "	Sent reply re lorries — only two lorries capable of carrying 35 cwt to 2 Tons (these refer only to 30 cwt lorries.	
11th "	Office routine	

1247 W 3299 200,000 (E) 8/14 J.B.C. & A. Forms/C. 2118/11.

Instructions regarding War Diaries and Intelligence Summaries are contained in F. S. Regs., Part II. and the Staff Manual respectively. Title pages will be prepared in manuscript.

WAR DIARY
or
INTELLIGENCE SUMMARY
(Erase heading not required.)

Army Form C. 2118.

Hour, Date, Place	Summary of Events and Information	Remarks and references to Appendices
12th April	Two consignments of cardamums amounting in all to 18,400 lbs for this Division only arrived at Railhead 2 oz per man were issued & 10 ounces retained. The rest sent back to the Base. The Base will be asked to send up as required. About 1 oz per week or at most 2 oz would appear sufficient.	
	Routine duties	
13th April	Arranged in AIRE with A D S & T for despatch of mules replaced by large Ordnance mules for Cavalry Regt Amtn. Reserve. To be entrained at AIRE & to bring only residue of that day's rations &c. The new mules came with halters & nose bags only. Mules going back to have same. Ropes for Ry Carriages had to be provided by local purchase.	
	Went round B.T.O's & saw mules & ascertained final figures for the despatch of Indian mules to Base.	
	Capt Bell Murray returned to the Dn. from duty to Marseilles with mules.	
14th April	The Coal mines once again have raised coal rates – to 40 francs per thousand kilos	
	D.S.C. directed to readjust the loading tables to the order to load net 30 cwt dis regarding equipment of lorries	
	Capt Bell Murray is to take next party of mules to Base.	
15th April	Ry carts came in from Batteries – 6 – 4 unserviceable, Bhartpur carts may be sent to A.T. Base as they may yield components of some use.	
	O/C D S C submitted a scheme for getting lorries over damaged roads – sent this on to Corps H.Q. with request for its return.	

Army Form C. 2118.

WAR DIARY
or
INTELLIGENCE SUMMARY

(Erase heading not required.)

Instructions regarding War Diaries and Intelligence Summaries are contained in F. S. Regs., Part II. and the Staff Manual respectively. Title pages will be prepared in manuscript.

Hour, Date, Place	Summary of Events and Information	Remarks and references to Appendices
16th April	Divisional Staff Ride —	
17th April	Routine duties New Transport officers appointed. Capt Sanders DSO. Capt A S Noake, Capt A L Hunt + Capt T F Brook. all S&TC. Went to Lucknow Bde + saw (with ADS&T) the new large mules being fitted with old saddles &c left when Indian mules were replaced. Saddles fit nicely with a little alteration of panel stuffing — also breast pieces but breechings are too short + girths ditto. Webbing purchased in AIRE is being fitted with the old buckles + leather pieces. This saddlery is to be replaced by Home Ordnance pattern before long.	
18th April	Jam supply now much more varied. Honey issued in lieu of jam was very much appreciated. — It is noteworthy how greatly an occasional variation is enjoyed. Inspected carts of Ammunition Col (S.A.A. Section) + decided on the move of 2 AT carts to Tr. H.Q. prior to handing them to the Ambulances. Saw the Field Squadron R.E. route marching, animals in good trim + harness well fitted	
19th April.	Routine duties. The strengths of 'B' Echelon are very varied in the Brigades statements. Mainly in excess of standard numbers. Queried these. It is worth noting that road space questions arise in connection with B Echelon every day of moves + the time for using any given road may be far too little unless the length of B Echelon is lessened.	

1247 W 3299 200,000 (E) 8/14 J.B.C. & A. Forms/C. 2118/11.

Instructions regarding War Diaries and Intelligence Summaries are contained in F. S. Regs., Part II. and the Staff Manual respectively. Title pages will be prepared in manuscript.

WAR DIARY
or
INTELLIGENCE SUMMARY
(Erase heading not required.)

Army Form C. 2118.

Hour, Date, Place	Summary of Events and Information	Remarks and references to Appendices
20th April	Office routine.	
21st "	Visited Railhead.	
22nd "	Inspected Ammunition mules of LUCKNOW Bde. The saddles are too small for these big mules (15 hands) but the alterations have been carried out satisfactorily & will do till the new saddlery arrives.	
23rd "	Inspected portion of Ammunition Column. AT Carts in very good order. Three AT Carts surplus which I ordered to be transferred to F Ambulances (one to each) to complete requirements.	
	[illegible] the [illegible] is sure to [illegible]	

1247 W 3299 200,000 (E) 8/14 J.B.C. & A. Forms/C. 2118/11.

Instructions regarding War Diaries and Intelligence Summaries are contained in F. S. Regs., Part II. and the Staff Manual respectively. Title pages will be prepared in manuscript.

WAR DIARY
or
INTELLIGENCE SUMMARY

(Erase heading not required.)

Army Form C. 2118.

Hour, Date, Place	Summary of Events and Information	Remarks and references to Appendices
	the [illegible] [illegible] resting on the [illegible]. Recd orders at 5.25 pm [illegible] Div [illegible] moving [illegible] S.E. of the [illegible] road & billet within the limits MAISON BLANCHE, STAPLE exclusive ST MARIE CAPPEL inclusive EXCLAORE inclusive RAVINGHOVE [illegible] transport of LUCKNOW [illegible] Bde [illegible] independently. 9 [illegible] [illegible] [illegible] of transport of LUCKNOW Bde & Divl troops. Starting pt [illegible] ESTREE BLANCHE [illegible] Railway [illegible] [illegible] [illegible] [illegible] take the [illegible] to [illegible] [illegible] [illegible] 7.30 pm. At 9.15 pm [illegible] [illegible] [illegible] first block [illegible] Corps [illegible] [illegible] which shd have been well clear, troops [illegible] the Brigade [illegible] [illegible] [illegible] stopped the [illegible] [illegible] for nearly 2 [illegible] up [illegible] [illegible] [illegible]. At 11 pm we [illegible] [illegible] [illegible] for 2 miles & [illegible] stopped [illegible] [illegible]	

1247 W 3299 200,000 (E) 8/14 J.B.C. & A. Forms/C. 2118/11.

Instructions regarding War Diaries and Intelligence Summaries are contained in F. S. Regs., Part II. and the Staff Manual respectively. Title pages will be prepared in manuscript.

WAR DIARY
or
INTELLIGENCE SUMMARY
(Erase heading not required.)

Army Form C. 2118.

Hour, Date, Place	Summary of Events and Information	Remarks and references to Appendices
	for 1½ hours by blocks in front & the breaking down of a G.S Wagon of Jodhpur Lancers (Corps troops). & eventually arrived at ST MARIE CAPPELLE (Divl Hd Qrs) at 7.30 AM. Distance about 18 miles. One AT cart backed into a ditch but was got out without much delay otherwise our transport moved well. The great fault was in want of communication between T.O's & Bde T.O's & the Sc. Column. I have issued special orders on this subject. Rendezvous for Supply Column was at STAPLE at 9 P.M	
25th April	Orders to stand ready to move at one hours notice. Rendezvous for Supply Column at LONGUE CROIX at 6 P.M	

1247 W 3299 200,000 (E) 8/14 J.B.C. & A. Forms/C. 2118/11.

Instructions regarding War Diaries and Intelligence Summaries are contained in F. S. Regs., Part II. and the Staff Manual respectively. Title pages will be prepared in manuscript.

WAR DIARY
or
INTELLIGENCE SUMMARY
(Erase heading not required.)

Army Form C. 2118.

Hour, Date, Place	Summary of Events and Information	Remarks and references to Appendices
26th April	Halt.	
27th "	Halt	
28th "	Division moved to WATOU. Recd orders to mass & park 'B' Echelon of Division in ST MARIE CHAPPELLE. Transport was parked by 3 P.M. Horses were taken out & placed in fields by Brigades. Orders given to be ready to march at ½ hours notice. Recd notice late in evening that horses would bring back rations. Horses arrived at 1.30 AM (29th) & rations were moved before 2 AM.	
29th "	Recd orders at 3.25 P.M. that transport was to move to WATOU. HQ of Division left at 4.10 P.M. One G.S. Wagon of R.D. Guards broke down on a hill necessitating wagons in rear halting on hill for 15 minutes	

1247 W 3299 200,000 (E) 8/14 J.B.C. & A. Forms/C. 2118/11.

Instructions regarding War Diaries and Intelligence Summaries are contained in F. S. Regs., Part II. and the Staff Manual respectively. Title pages will be prepared in manuscript.

WAR DIARY
or
INTELLIGENCE SUMMARY
(Erase heading not required.)

Army Form C. 2118.

Hour, Date, Place	Summary of Events and Information	Remarks and references to Appendices
30th April	Arrived at WATOU at 8 P.M. but owing to Supply Column Lorries not having left the transport was halted till about 9.30 P.M. Halted at WATOU.	
	H. Carrington Lt Colonel O/C. A.S.C. 1st I. Cavy Divn	

1247 W 3299 200,000 (E) 8/14 J.B.C. & A. Forms/C. 2118/11.

Army Form C. 2118.

Instructions regarding War Diaries and Intelligence Summaries are contained in F. S. Regs., Part II. and the Staff Manual respectively. Title pages will be prepared in manuscript.

WAR DIARY
or
INTELLIGENCE SUMMARY
(Erase heading not required.)

Hour, Date, Place	Summary of Events and Information	Remarks and references to Appendices
1st May	Halted at WATOU.	
2nd "	Received orders to march back to billets previously occupied at ST MARIE CHAPPELLE & vicinity. The Arts [?] of B Echelon marched under my command at 8.30 a.m. The large number of men & horses marching with B Echelon was brought to notice on the march up. The numbers were reduced on this march by about 296 men & 340 animals. The line occupied 2 miles. It was noticed that buckets etc were fastened in rear of GS Wagons which interfered with working of rear brake — orders issued to stop this. A better system of communication from ~~front to~~ rear to front of Echelon was introduced. Every hour a "March report" was submitted by T.O. to [?] Brigade	

1247 W 3299 200,000 (E) 8/14 J.B.C. & A. Forms/C. 2118/11.

Instructions regarding War Diaries and Intelligence Summaries are contained in F. S. Regs., Part II. and the Staff Manual respectively. Title pages will be prepared in manuscript.

WAR DIARY
or
INTELLIGENCE SUMMARY
(Erase heading not required.)

Army Form C. 2118.

Hour, Date, Place	Summary of Events and Information	Remarks and references to Appendices
	giving distances lost between units & the Brigade transport in front. This was passed on by Regtl T.O's to Bde T.O's who entered their reports & handed in to O.C. Column. This saved a good deal of passing up & down the line & only entailed the writing of a few words by T.O's. Pace of Column 2½ miles an hour.	
3rd May	Halted at ST MARIE CHAPPELLE.	
4th "	Ditto	
5th "	The Division marched back to billets with H.Q. at ROQUETOIRE	
6th "	Halt	
7th "	Halt	
8th "	Halt	

1247 W 3299 200,000 (E) 8/14 J.B.C. & A. Forms/C. 2118/11.

Instructions regarding War Diaries and Intelligence Summaries are contained in F. S. Regs., Part II. and the Staff Manual respectively. Title pages will be prepared in manuscript.

WAR DIARY
or
INTELLIGENCE SUMMARY
(Erase heading not required.)

Army Form C. 2118.

Hour, Date, Place	Summary of Events and Information	Remarks and references to Appendices
9th May	Division ordered to be ready to move at 2 hours notice. Warned that all baggage will be dropped at selected places & left under a guard. The empty B Echelon wagons to be dealt with by administrative orders from Corps Hd Qrs. The present intention is to send them to AIRE to take 2 days special orders & rations from barges moored on the canal. These supplies will then be made down to join Division to move in either of the following ways:— (a) Carried forward in G.S. Wagons in advance permit these wagons to move, although to be free motor traffic. (b) Transferred to improvised pack transport if roads are too bad to permit wheels to move on them	

Instructions regarding War Diaries and Intelligence Summaries are contained in F. S. Regs., Part II. and the Staff Manual respectively. Title pages will be prepared in manuscript.

WAR DIARY
or
INTELLIGENCE SUMMARY
(Erase heading not required.)

Army Form C. 2118.

Hour, Date, Place	Summary of Events and Information	Remarks and references to Appendices
	Special scale	
	British — Indian — Animals	* tinned mutton
	lbs. oz — lbs. oz	
	Biscuits 1. 0 — 1. 8	
	Presd Meat 1. 0 — [illegible]*	
	Tea 5/8 — 1/3	Only tea to cook
	Sugar 2	
	Gur – — 3	
	Jam or [illegible] 2	
	Salt – — 1/2	
	Hay — — 6 lbs } per animal	
	Oats — — 12 [illegible] }	
	Gross Weight 2 - 10 — 2. 0	
	Of animals for employment with transport	
	British Regt. 18 Pack horses at [illegible]	
	Indian 18	
10th May	Approx distance	

Instructions regarding War Diaries and Intelligence Summaries are contained in F. S. Regs., Part II. and the Staff Manual respectively. Title pages will be prepared in manuscript.

WAR DIARY
or
INTELLIGENCE SUMMARY
(Erase heading not required.)

Army Form C. 2118.

Hour, Date, Place	Summary of Events and Information	Remarks and references to Appendices
11th May	Office routine	
12th "	" "	
13th "	Div! Comdr inspected [illegible] [illegible] mules with the [illegible]. The pack saddles (of the AT Mules [illegible]) were made too small & the large size will be obtained as soon as possible	
14th "	Office routine.	
15th "	Went round [illegible] & explained to B.T.O's the new transport to relieve the remaining Indian transport. Arranged for the latter to be collected at ROQUETOIRE when available.	
16th "	Received information that new transport would arrive at ARQUES about 1 P.M. Ordered all B.T.O's & R.T.O's to be present & arrived myself at ARQUES at 1 P.M. Transport arrived correct for all units except RHA Batteries	

1247 W 3299 200,000 (E) 8/14 J.B.C. & A. Forms/C. 2118/11.

Instructions regarding War Diaries and Intelligence Summaries are contained in F. S. Regs., Part II. and the Staff Manual respectively. Title pages will be prepared in manuscript.

WAR DIARY
or
INTELLIGENCE SUMMARY
(Erase heading not required.)

Army Form C. 2118.

Hour, Date, Place	Summary of Events and Information	Remarks and references to Appendices
	& Divl. Ammunition Column. The transport consisted of Limbered G.S. Wagons with teams of four mules (rider + driver) in place of L.D. Horses. The mules are fine animals about 15 hands & very quiet.	
	Issued orders for all Indian transport to be collected at ROQUETOIRE tomorrow by 5 P.M. & handed over to T.O. Divl Troops.	
	1 NCO now doing duty with Transport H^d^ Q^rs^ of each Brigade & Divl Troops to proceed with the transport.	
	The following is the new transport received	

	Limbered GS Wagons	Horses Riding	Mules D	Regtl Drivers	ASC Drivers	
17th Lancers	5	1	20	10	—	
8th Hussars	5	1	20	11	—	+ 1 Sergt
KDG's	5	1	20	11	—	+ 1 Cpl

Instructions regarding War Diaries and Intelligence Summaries are contained in F. S. Regs., Part II. and the Staff Manual respectively. Title pages will be prepared in manuscript.

WAR DIARY
or
INTELLIGENCE SUMMARY
(Erase heading not required.)

Army Form C. 2118.

Hour, Date, Place	Summary of Events and Information	Remarks and references to Appendices

	Light G.S.	[illegible]	[illegible] D.	Regt Drivers	ASC Drivers
6 Indian Regts	20	6	120	—	60
3 F. Ambulances	7	3	37	—	21
Div Hd Qrs	1	—	4	—	2
3 Bde Hd Qrs	3	—	12	—	6
3 Mob Vety Secns	3	—	12	—	6

17th May — The 1st Army having taken the enemy's lines of [illegible] the Indian Cavy Corps [less B. Echelon] was ordered to move to a position of readiness about LE MARCHET [illegible] 1st Cavy Divn [illegible] Hd Qrs & 2 Bdes ALLOUAGNE & 1 Bde [illegible] F. BURBURRE. Supply Column ordered [illegible] about midnight. B Echelon of Bdes was collected at one place in each Brigade area from which troops had moved & that of Divl troops at ROCQUETOIRE. All wagons ready loaded to march at 2 hrs notice under Offr ASC

~~18th May~~

18th May — Position as on night of 17th. Proceeded to Hd Qrs to inspect A Echelon. Found a good many mules

Instructions regarding War Diaries and Intelligence Summaries are contained in F. S. Regs., Part II. and the Staff Manual respectively. Title pages will be prepared in manuscript.

WAR DIARY
or
INTELLIGENCE SUMMARY
(Erase heading not required.)

Army Form C. 2118.

Hour, Date, Place	Summary of Events and Information	Remarks and references to Appendices
	galled behind the elbows (most of them the mounts arrived with). Some of the galls were due to faulty position of surcingle buckle which I gave orders about.	
19th May	Proceeded to Hd Qrs to interview AA & QMG & attended a meeting of GOC & Bde Majors when the question of reduction of followers was discussed. The result: reduced followers to a minimum of per Unit:—	
	1 Syce per B. officer provided he rides his master's 2nd horse & leads the pack horse (A Echelon)	
	6 Private Servants to come as riders for horses (A Echelon)	
	4 Sweepers (A Echelon)	
	Of the above 2 will be carried in [illegible] cart & 2 in L. G. S. Wagon of each squadron	
	6 Private servants 2 Mochis 1 Mistri 8 Cooks 4 Sweepers } B Echelon	

1247 W 3299 200,000 (E) 8/14 J.B.C. & A. Forms/C. 2118/11.

Instructions regarding War Diaries and Intelligence Summaries are contained in F. S. Regs., Part II. and the Staff Manual respectively. Title pages will be prepared in manuscript.

WAR DIARY
or
INTELLIGENCE SUMMARY
(Erase heading not required.)

Army Form C. 2118.

Hour, Date, Place	Summary of Events and Information	Remarks and references to Appendices
	All followers with B Echelon will move on foot	
	All other followers to be evacuated.	
	All men who were necessary to return to former billets.	
20th May	Office routine	
21st "	" "	
22nd "	Six drivers ASC with new transport were trained to ride & drive 8 drivers (12) were withdrawn from each Unit leaving 3 of the old drivers who had been trained previously to ride & drive. Units have now	
	British Regts 3 ASC drivers 18 Regtl drivers & 1 Regtl N.C.O	
	Indian " 14 ASC drivers 7 Regtl drivers & 1 ASC N.C.O.	
	Attended inspection of transport of 29th Lancers by G.O.C. Divn. There had not been time	

Instructions regarding War Diaries and Intelligence Summaries are contained in F. S. Regs., Part II. and the Staff Manual respectively. Title pages will be prepared in manuscript.

WAR DIARY
or
INTELLIGENCE SUMMARY
(Erase heading not required.)

Army Form C. 2118.

Hour, Date, Place	Summary of Events and Information	Remarks and references to Appendices
	to fit the harness properly but progress has been made.	
23rd May	Surplus ASC drivers sent to railhead	
24th "	Office routine	
25th "	Inspected transport of LUCKNOW Bde. Gave instructions to be careful that mules were tightly girthed also when necessary to hold back girths by means of surcingle & a baggage strap	
26th "	Was informed that LD mules to replace HD Horses (4 LD mules to replace 2 HD Horses) might arrive today. Made necessary arrangements but no orders arrived.	
27th "	Division marched to area of LONGUE CROIX, QUEUE D'OXELAERE, EYHOUCK, LENIEPPE, EBBLINGHAM. A Echelon Transport accompanied Brigades. This was the first time A Echelon was equipped	

1247 W 3299 200,000 (E) 8/14 J.B.C. & A. Forms/C. 2118/11.

Instructions regarding War Diaries and Intelligence Summaries are contained in F. S. Regs., Part II. and the Staff Manual respectively. Title pages will be prepared in manuscript.

WAR DIARY
or
INTELLIGENCE SUMMARY
(Erase heading not required.)

Army Form C. 2118.

Hour, Date, Place	Summary of Events and Information	Remarks and references to Appendices
	with first moving transport. [illegible] Post [illegible]	
	1 Water cart with one pair L.D. Horses	* 1 in place of Maltese cart not available
	1 Cooks " " two pairs " "	
	*5 Limbered G.S. Wagons with two pairs L.D. Horses	
	The transport kept up well.	
	'B' Echelon followed route allotted to Brigades.	
	Report Centre open at STAPLE at 10 a.m.	
28th May	Division marched to billetting area West of the line NOORPEENE – SEINEHOUCK – East of the ~~line~~ road L'ERRELSBRUGGE – LEDERZEELE	
	Billetting areas —	
	AMBALA Bde – SEINEHOUCK – CRAYHILL – BALEMBERG – NOORDPEENE.	
	SIALKOTE Bde X roads S. of POINT DU JOUR.	
	X roads N of LE LONG CHAMP – BROXEELE	
	LUCKNOW Bde EIRRELSBRUGGE – HOGENHIL – X roads one mile W of SEINEHOUK	

1247 W 3299 200,000 (E) 8/14 J.B.C. & A. Forms/C. 2118/11.

Army Form C. 2118.

Instructions regarding War Diaries and Intelligence Summaries are contained in F. S. Regs., Part II. and the Staff Manual respectively. Title pages will be prepared in manuscript.

WAR DIARY
or
INTELLIGENCE SUMMARY
(Erase heading not required.)

Hour, Date, Place	Summary of Events and Information	Remarks and references to Appendices
	Divl. Troops RUBROUCK - DOORAERT - BALEMBERG	
	Divl. Hd Qrs RUBROUCK.	
	B Echelon of Division [illegible] under my command.	
	900 [illegible] men from each Bde + 3 F. Coys [illegible] detailed for duty in Trenches near YPRES. Proceeded ~~there~~ to VLAMERTINGHE [illegible] [illegible] + were [illegible] [illegible] for night	
	Seven lorries were detailed for supply [illegible] [illegible] [illegible] - RENDEZVOUS RENINGHELST at 5 P.M. Orders were [illegible] [illegible] that the lorries [illegible] proceed up to the [illegible] where the supplies were dumped. It was [illegible] [illegible] intended that A Echelon Limbered Wagons [illegible] meet lorries at Rendezvous.	
	Rendezvous for remainder of Division at	

BALEMBERG at 5 P.M.

Instructions regarding War Diaries and Intelligence Summaries are contained in F. S. Regs., Part II. and the Staff Manual respectively. Title pages will be prepared in manuscript.

WAR DIARY
or
INTELLIGENCE SUMMARY
(Erase heading not required.)

Army Form C. 2118.

Hour, Date, Place	Summary of Events and Information	Remarks and references to Appendices
29th May	Office routine.	
30th "	Recd information that 66 L.D. Mules wd arrive for Division in place of H.D. Horses. These are sufficient for 3 Regts @ 22 each. Handed over to K.D.G's 29th Lancers & 36th Jacob's Horse	
31st "	Interviewed ADS&T re disposal of H.D. Horses (42) & was told to send them to AIRE being required for 1st Army	
31st "	Issued orders for H D Horses to be marched to AIRE at 6 am 1st June & to arrive before 4 PM. Actual number reported fit to go 39.	

H. Carrington Lt Col
O/C ASC 1st I. Cav Divn

1247 W 3299 200,000 (E) 8/14 J.B.C. & A. Forms/C. 2118/11.

Instructions regarding War Diaries and Intelligence Summaries are contained in F. S. Regs., Part II. and the Staff Manual respectively. Title pages will be prepared in manuscript.

WAR DIARY
or
INTELLIGENCE SUMMARY
(Erase heading not required.)

Army Form C. 2118.

Hour, Date, Place	Summary of Events and Information	Remarks and references to Appendices
1st June	Routine work.	
2nd "	" "	
3rd "	Received intimation that L.D. Mules in place of H.D. Horses will arrive tomorrow at ARNEKE for following:— Div^l H^d Q^rs 3 B^de H^d Q^rs 6 Reg^ts For this reason only the Ambulances to be equipped. Went round to B^de T. Officers & gave necessary instructions In the afternoon received other comments w^d arrive at 19.10. B.T.O.s were present at Station & animals taken over. In addition w^d come two 2 H Limbered Wagons for — one for Signal Squadron 1st Div^n & one for Signal Squadron 2nd Div^n	
4th "	Visited Brigades to see new mules.	

1247 W 3299 200,000 (E) 8/14 J.B.C. & A. Forms/C. 2118/11.

Instructions regarding War Diaries and Intelligence Summaries are contained in F. S. Regs., Part II. and the Staff Manual respectively. Title pages will be prepared in manuscript.

WAR DIARY
or
INTELLIGENCE SUMMARY
(Erase heading not required.)

Army Form C. 2118.

Hour, Date, Place	Summary of Events and Information	Remarks and references to Appendices
5th ~~May~~ June	Despatched 98 [illegible] H.D. ([illegible] [illegible] [illegible] [illegible] by D. [illegible]) – 18 ASC [illegible] to AIRE. Sgt. Taylor [illegible] [illegible] [illegible] [illegible] & posted to UMBALLA [illegible] in place of Sergt Newman	
6th June	Office routine.	
7th "	39 L.D. Mules & 21 ASC drivers arrived at ARNEKE for Fd Ambulances	
8th "	Desp. Detail 26 L.D. [illegible] under Sgt. Hollis for LUCKNOW & SIALKOT [illegible] [illegible] the [illegible] with orders to collect 20 H.D. Horses & [illegible] them to AIRE stopping at STAPLE night of 9th. Also 10 H.D. Horses to join [illegible] at STAPLE on evening of 9th.	
9th "	Office routine.	

1247 W 3299 200,000 (E) 8/14 J.B.C. & A. Forms/C. 2118/11.

Instructions regarding War Diaries and Intelligence Summaries are contained in F. S. Regs., Part II. and the Staff Manual respectively. Title pages will be prepared in manuscript.

WAR DIARY

or

INTELLIGENCE SUMMARY

(Erase heading not required.)

Army Form C. 2118.

Hour, Date, Place	Summary of Events and Information	Remarks and references to Appendices
10th June 11th " 12th " 13th " 14th "	Routine work.	
	Inspected B Echelon Transport of UMBALLA Bde. Harness of new waggons wanted fitting with exception of 8th Hussars.	
15th "	The whole of the Division moved to original billeting area with Divl H.Qrs at ROCQUETOIRE. The number of followers with 19th Lancers is close on 40 or double the number allowed to march with B Echelon. These Regts waggons were badly loaded & the [illegible] could not be carried owing to [illegible] being fastened to rear of waggons. Had these all thrown away & reported in writing to AA & QMG.	

1247 W 3299 200,000 (E) 8/14 J.B.C. & A. Forms/C. 2118/11.

Instructions regarding War Diaries and Intelligence Summaries are contained in F. S. Regs., Part II. and the Staff Manual respectively. Title pages will be prepared in manuscript.

WAR DIARY
or
INTELLIGENCE SUMMARY
(Erase heading not required.)

Army Form C. 2118.

Hour, Date, Place	Summary of Events and Information	Remarks and references to Appendices
16th June	Routine.	
17th "	"	
18th "	Inspected transport of LUCKNOW Bde.	
19th "	Routine	
20th "	Inspected transport of SIALKOTE Bde. All very well turned out.	
21st "	Routine	
22nd "	Reconnoitred roads round AIRE with a view to the Div.n drawing supplies from Berguette on the canal. Selected suitable roads	
23rd "	Routine	
24th	"	
25th	"	
26th	"	
27th	"	
28th	"	

1247 W 3299 200,000 (E) 8/14 J.B.C. & A. Forms/C. 2118/11.

Instructions regarding War Diaries and Intelligence Summaries are contained in F. S. Regs., Part II. and the Staff Manual respectively. Title pages will be prepared in manuscript.

WAR DIARY
or
INTELLIGENCE SUMMARY

(Erase heading not required.)

Army Form C. 2118.

Hour, Date, Place	Summary of Events and Information	Remarks and references to Appendices
29th June	A digging party consisting of Field Squadron, Field Troop, Det-nt 6th Cavy, 19th Lancers & 17th Lancers, proceeded to join Indian Corps.	

Strength

	British	Indian	Animals
1st Squadron	197	–	199
Troop	18	142	96
6th Cavy	5	255	–
17th Lancers	259	–	–
19th "	5	255	–
Total	484	652	295

The Dismounted men were conveyed into motor buses (?). The horses proceeded practically up to billets + 2 GS Wagons were lent by Brigade Divn to each Cavy Det-nt.

Time leaving at Rendezvous — LE LOBE 11 AM & saw them distributed.

1247 W 3299 200,000 (E) 8/14 J.B.C. & A. Forms/C. 2118/11.

Army Form C. 2118.

WAR DIARY
or
INTELLIGENCE SUMMARY
(Erase heading not required.)

Instructions regarding War Diaries and Intelligence Summaries are contained in F. S. Regs., Part II. and the Staff Manual respectively. Title pages will be prepared in manuscript.

Hour, Date, Place	Summary of Events and Information	Remarks and references to Appendices
30th June	Proceeded to see arrangements for rations for digging parties were correctly issued. [illegible] Lt Col O/C ASC 1st I. Cav. Div.	

1247 W 3299 200,000 (E) 8/14 J.B.C. & A. Forms/C. 2118/11.

Instructions regarding War Diaries and Intelligence Summaries are contained in F. S. Regs., Part II. and the Staff Manual respectively. Title pages will be prepared in manuscript.

WAR DIARY
or
INTELLIGENCE SUMMARY
(Erase heading not required.)

Army Form C. 2118.

Hour, Date, Place	Summary of Events and Information	Remarks and references to Appendices
1st July	Visited Railhead & Supply Officer Umballa Bde	
2nd "	Visited Railhead. Saw AD of ST with reference to establishment of drivers with Fd Ambulances; also on subject of emergency ration for horses (1lb grain). It was found that wastage occurred owing to heat & other causes as the ration was not in tins & therefore that in time it wd have to be replaced. ADST informed me that it had been decided that no further issue wd be made.	
3rd July	Umballa Bde relieved Sialkote Bde (digging party attached to Indian Corps). Lorries for Detnt of FOSSE were not permitted to cross the bridge so rations were dumped on side of LOCON-LESTREM Rd using the door refilling point of MEERUT DIVISION which was clear earlier in the day.	

1247 W 3299 200,000 (E) 8/14 J.B.C. & A. Forms/C. 2118/11.

Army Form C. 2118.

Instructions regarding War Diaries and Intelligence Summaries are contained in F. S. Regs., Part II. and the Staff Manual respectively. Title pages will be prepared in manuscript.

WAR DIARY
or
INTELLIGENCE SUMMARY
(Erase heading not required.)

Hour, Date, Place	Summary of Events and Information	Remarks and references to Appendices
4th July	Visited Railhead also digging parties.	
5th "	Visited Railhead.	
6th "	Visited Railhead	
7th "	Visited Railhead. LUCKNOW Bde relieved UMBALLA Bde (digging party) Strength of party moved as follows:-	

	British	Ind.	Animals
K.D.G.'s	320	-	-
36th Jacobs H.	10	315	2
29th Lancers	10	315	2
Fd Sqdn	200	-	200
Fd Troop	10	130	96
	553	760	300
Supply Estmt	5		
	558	760	300

1247 W 3299 200,000 (E) 8/14 J.B.C. & A. Forms/C. 2118/11.

Instructions regarding War Diaries and Intelligence Summaries are contained in F. S. Regs., Part II. and the Staff Manual respectively. Title pages will be prepared in manuscript.

WAR DIARY
or
INTELLIGENCE SUMMARY
(Erase heading not required.)

Army Form C. 2118.

Hour, Date, Place	Summary of Events and Information	Remarks and references to Appendices
8th July.	S.S.O. returned from leave last night. Routine duties. O/C ASC 2nd Dn consulted this Dn with regard to provision of proper proportion of spare drivers & animals for Tr of Field Ambulances which are much below 10%.	
9th July	O/C ASC ~~goes~~ on 7 days leave & therefore handed charge to SSO. Visited Railhead and recorded ½ margin reports asked for the previous week. Salt has been over purchased for horses in Ambala Bde up to 1 oz & beyond the authorised ½ oz per animal. This is stopped now that rock salt is coming up regularly.	
10th July	Visited AA&QMG regarding (a) Apples from N. Zealand (b) 29 horses LD come up in exchange for H.D. in routine way (not specially dealt with by AD S&T) This completes us in LD animals tho some HD are not evacuated owing to want of R.D harness (breast) AA&QMG was reminded of this point & is dealing with it himself (c) Rations (oats) for Indn Cav: horses under 15 hds ½ in — (d) Issued dones & rations — AD S&T informed me that a conference tomorrow night - probably - decide to give these free so that the pending correspondence might well be delayed 48 hours — AA&QMG informed (e) Gur emergency ration for horses — now fermented, melted, lost &c in many cases & can not be drawn afresh — I suggested that as Indian F S ration includes only 1 oz gur & we give 3 oz daily Regts really might manage to maintain the horse ration intact by steady turnover. This was noted in connection with the Barge Scheme. Issued orders to SO Dn Troops, O/C DSC & DAP regarding records of rations drawn from Railhead & purchased locally. These units are from 1st July dealt with as Dn Troops but exceptionally. The procedure is clumsy as regards the former who necessarily are constantly in immediate touch with Railhead & must often purchase at some distance from S.O. Dn Troops position with his other units.	

1247 W 3299 200,000 (E) 8/14 J.B.C. & A. Forms/C. 2118/11.

Instructions regarding War Diaries and Intelligence Summaries are contained in F. S. Regs., Part II. and the Staff Manual respectively. Title pages will be prepared in manuscript.

WAR DIARY
or
INTELLIGENCE SUMMARY
(Erase heading not required.)

Army Form C. 2118.

Hour, Date, Place	Summary of Events and Information	Remarks and references to Appendices
11th July	Capt Whittell came in from Dysjey Party – reports all smoothly working. Went to Railhead & found one wagon of meat, bread & groceries cut off en route – issues made up of M & V Rations, Iron Grocery rations & local balances. Bacon tasted by me & found of highly satisfactory quality in all samples I saw. Certain billets changed. Official list now up to date came in this evening.	
12th July	29 L D horses arrived on 10.7.15 for 3 Batteries RHA. Amtn Coln & 7 Troop. A similar number of H D Horses now ordered to be evacuated to 1st Army Remount Section at GONNEHEM. Visited Railhead – all correct. Saw ADS & T on several points. (a) Conference yesterday & it was settled that rations & forage is to be issued free to Gendarmes without any question of recovery of value from the French Govt – letter No 266 sent out (dated 13.7.15) These settled questions of certificates. (b) Conference settled that O/c ASC is exclusively director of all Supply and Transport services within a Dn & that SSO is an assistant for supplies. (c) A new S.O's Diary Form has been settled on. (d) M T Corps (Amtn Parks & DS Cols) may arrange supplies & purchases in the usual way under SSO without intervention of a BSO & they use their Imprest a/c for Supplies as well as for Pay. (e) Condensed Milk is to be issued at times as a substitute for frozen meat only – i.e. not for tinned meat – British Troops only.	

Instructions regarding War Diaries and Intelligence Summaries are contained in F. S. Regs., Part II. and the Staff Manual respectively. Title pages will be prepared in manuscript.

WAR DIARY
or
INTELLIGENCE SUMMARY
(Erase heading not required.)

Army Form C. 2118.

Hour, Date, Place	Summary of Events and Information	Remarks and references to Appendices
	(f) Requisitioning Rules and rules for rationing French with attached to British Formations are to be issued. (g) Question of increasing spare L D Horses & Drivers with Field Ambces is being considered on representation of 2nd D.C.D. Saw BTO's – no particular points at issue. Saw RO Lucknow Bde who is puzzled as to purchases of green fodder which is now drying. He was told to record the purchases as made & not to record hay (which is forbidden) as green fodder. He must issue however partly dried fodder at green equivalent. Capt Shaw reports arrival to replace Lt Hubbard as O/C Echelon DSC & did duty today as O/C.	
13.7.15.	Complaint as to BREAD being broken in transit & unfit for human consumption sent in for 2nd time by Major Evans RE. No other unit has complained! It is known to me that 2% approx are broken in transit. This had better be thoro'ly gone into. Letter to all SO's asking for 7 days definite figures. To ADS&T asking for independant examination at Railhead & explaining the circumstances. Reply to BSO at the Dyeing Party. At Railhead 1 truck containing Groceries, meat & bread cut off en route. Such out of wagons go to a collecting centre now & are not made good to Railhead. Therefore tinned meat, biscuits & miscellaneous groceries & substitutes were issued from Railhead & from Barges.	

1247 W 3299 200,000 (E) 8/14 J.B.C. & A. Forms/C. 2118/11.

Instructions regarding War Diaries and Intelligence Summaries are contained in F. S. Regs., Part II. and the Staff Manual respectively. Title pages will be prepared in manuscript.

WAR DIARY
or
INTELLIGENCE SUMMARY

(Erase heading not required.)

Army Form C. 2118.

Hour, Date, Place	Summary of Events and Information	Remarks and references to Appendices
14.7.15	Went via BETHUNE to ESTAIRES to see the rations dumped for Digging Parties. Examined bread in Lorries & recorded statistics of damaged Loaves. Whittell tells me loaves generally burned on top but sodden except in centre. This comes from sacking them before they are cool & stacking them in Trucks whilst new & soft. No other [illegible] complaints & a consensus of praise of the bread exists. I am inclined to think the proportions of broken loaves & sackfuls which are not wholly satisfactory are an inconvenience which is real but exaggerated & also might be lessened by care & slight variations. This will seem clearer when we have some definite figures — 7 days hence.	
	Saw AA+QMG's of Corps & Dn together and gathered that the economic aspect was fully recognised at G.H.Q. as amongst the important questions of the present & future and that the purchasing process worried too much. This Dn leads the rates and the units are [illegible] surpluses if they do not eat any of their rations. This is a routine process but it is so difficult to teach units that if other Dns have not continually rubbed it in as we have — & still have to — some waste must occur. — Horses grain is a difficulty —	
15.7.15.	Went to Railhead & took further bread statistics of damaged loaves. Saw ABS & T & CC. who shewed me rates of 2nd Dn & a letter to the O/C ASC. I promised to assist them when they applied.	
	SSO & I BSO & SO & T 2nd Dn came to consult re rates. I explained that we buy on system of stopping purchases if rates rise in one area & importing from another by intercommunication of BSOs — also by dealing in substitutes of one sort — of fodder say — rises in price. Also SO's inform each other of variations. The use of B echelon & S Wagons was explained. Also control by means of fixed rates. The whole thing however is due to the BSOs &	

Instructions regarding War Diaries and Intelligence Summaries are contained in F. S. Regs., Part II. and the Staff Manual respectively. Title pages will be prepared in manuscript.

WAR DIARY
or
INTELLIGENCE SUMMARY

(Erase heading not required.)

Army Form C. 2118.

Hour, Date, Place	Summary of Events and Information	Remarks and references to Appendices
	I have asked mine to assist 2nd Dn & have attempted to encourage them by letting them know ADS&T has observed their success. Whittell, Christie, Bowker & Heyland are in the order named very successful with the audit of their RO's.	
	AA&QMG sent in Digging Party new programme & orders went out to Bdes	
	Went to St MARTIN & saw Dl Amtn Park & will be there at inspection tomorrow	
	Went to D.S. Colm & wrote out orders for Digging Party arrangements in consultation with SO DS Colm at 10.30 p.m.	
16.7.15	Went to inspection of Dl Amtn Park by DA&QMG. Thence to Railhead – Meat ration reduced – Fresh from 1¼ lbs to 1 lb & Tinned from 12 oz to 9 oz. Mustard reduced from 1/20 to 1/50 oz daily and ⅓ tin of tinned milk & 1/10 gill lime juice (3 times weekly) are now extra issues current.	
	Saw S.O. Digging party who had received no strength statements – Gave him copy of scheme & later went round Bdes to get figures sent out to him.	
	Saw SO Ambala Bde who discussed purchases of potatoes &c & believes that Lucknow low rates due to low grades usually fed to animals being bought. He anticipates early rise of rates in which I concur. Lucknow Bde potatoes examined – seemed good sound supply & SO Sialkote Bde informed he may get some from Lucknow Bde (Fr 5.00 % kilos) if he approves of the quality.	
	Sent out reminder to SO's on several points which require looking into & which have recently arisen. KDG's grumbled about new potatoes turning colour when cooked – ordered Lucknow Bde SO to replace those not wholly satisfactory & will visit KDGs tomorrow & look into the case.	
	At 2 pm O/C DSC & SO came in to say that by a misreading of orders	

1247 W 3299 200,000 (E) 8/14 J.B.C. & A. Forms/C. 2118/11.

Instructions regarding War Diaries and Intelligence Summaries are contained in F. S. Regs., Part II. and the Staff Manual respectively. Title pages will be prepared in manuscript.

WAR DIARY

or

INTELLIGENCE SUMMARY

(Erase heading not required.)

Army Form C. 2118.

Hour, Date, Place	Summary of Events and Information	Remarks and references to Appendices
	Lorries loads were adjusted today as if for tomorrow — lorries held up pending orders to readjust loads. Orders readjustment at 2.15 & warned Bdes not to expect lorries till 5 pm but they got out correctly loaded at 4.20–4.30 pm. A good bit of work by S.O. Echelon of D.S.C. (Capt Byrch). I accepted onus for the misunderstood orders but the wording seemed clear & dates were all correct & the misunderstanding was due to a preconception which is not likely to recur. Discovered that delay in Sialkote Bde figures due to forgetfulness duly acknowledged by Bde Maj (new apptmt) — The scheme of reliefs not communicated to B.S.O. till next day — thus loading at Railhead was not accurate & must be readjusted — This is a nuisance & a difficult job if Div moving — the lesson occurred at a convenient time & no harm done. We have now virtually 4 Bdes & D.T. — S.S. Estab can just cope with this. — Col Codrington returns tonight & resumes command of ASC this Div.	
17th July	Routine work.	
18th "	Six Batteries have moved near THEROANNE arranged with AA & QMG that in event of Barge Scheme coming off, their baggage will be dumped at that place. A census of all Motor cars, motor ambulances & motor lorries was taken at 3.30 P.M.	

1247 W 3299 200,000 (E) 8/14 J.B.C. & A. Forms/C. 2118/11.

Instructions regarding War Diaries and Intelligence Summaries are contained in F. S. Regs., Part II. and the Staff Manual respectively. Title pages will be prepared in manuscript.

WAR DIARY
or
INTELLIGENCE SUMMARY

(Erase heading not required.)

Army Form C. 2118.

Hour, Date, Place	Summary of Events and Information	Remarks and references to Appendices
19th July	Sanctioned rec'd for Indian drivers of Amm'n Column (the British drivers having been trained) to replace 14 A.S.C. drivers & 1 N.C.O. with each Indian Cav'y Regt. – Havildars to replace the N.C.O. This leaves Indian Cavalry Regts with entire Indian Est'mt with exception of 1 British Shoeing Smith. The relieved A.S.C. drivers to be despatched to Base Horse Transport Dep't.	
20th "	It has been noticed that the split pin for connecting rods of limber [illegible] breaks frequently the rods trailing on the ground & breaking. Visited Ambala Fd Coy & inspected limbers & gave instructions for the [illegible] holding pin to be [illegible] & end of pin rivetted.	
21st	R.H.A. drivers distributed to Regts 1 Havildar 1 Naik & 13 drivers to each.	

Instructions regarding War Diaries and Intelligence Summaries are contained in F. S. Regs., Part II. and the Staff Manual respectively. Title pages will be prepared in manuscript.

WAR DIARY
or
INTELLIGENCE SUMMARY
(Erase heading not required.)

Army Form C. 2118.

Hour, Date, Place	Summary of Events and Information	Remarks and references to Appendices
22nd July	A.S.C. drivers returned by Regts & despatched to Base.	
23rd "	Conference at Corps H.Qrs. Present AA&QMG ADS&T. 2 O/C A.S.C. 2. S.S.Os & 2 Staff Captains. Subject: The signing of form & certificate by Q Branch weekly that the number of rations drawn during the week were correct. It was decided that Units shd enter their ration strength on B.213 & that Q Branch shd compare these figures with number of rations issued by S.O's. so as to form a check on figures given in B.55 to Supply officers.	
24th "	Recd orders for Major Haycraft, Bde S. Officer Sialkot Bde to proceed to Base Marseilles	

Instructions regarding War Diaries and Intelligence Summaries are contained in F. S. Regs., Part II. and the Staff Manual respectively. Title pages will be prepared in manuscript.

WAR DIARY
or
INTELLIGENCE SUMMARY
(Erase heading not required.)

Army Form C. 2118.

Hour, Date, Place	Summary of Events and Information	Remarks and references to Appendices
	& Capt. Wright to join Division from Marseilles Issued orders for Capt. Noake to relieve Major Hyland, Capt Wright on arrival to replace Capt Noake.	
25th ~~J~~	Inspection of Sialkote Bde Transport by Corps Commander who expressed his pleasure at the state of efficiency.	
25th July	Office routine. Major Hyland left for Marseilles	
26th "	Inspection of transport of LUCKNOW & AMBALLA Brigades by Corps Commander who complimented all concerned on the efficiency of the transport	
27th "	Inspected Ammunition Park. Their turn out well, lorries very clean & movements carried out quickly & well — a very efficient unit under Major Scott A.S. Corps	

1247 W 3299 200,000 (E) 8/14 J.B.C. & A. Forms/C. 2118/11.

Instructions regarding War Diaries and Intelligence Summaries are contained in F. S. Regs., Part II. and the Staff Manual respectively. Title pages will be prepared in manuscript.

WAR DIARY
or
INTELLIGENCE SUMMARY
(Erase heading not required.)

Army Form C. 2118.

Hour, Date, Place	Summary of Events and Information	Remarks and references to Appendices
28th July	Routine. Digging parties rejoined Division	
29th "	"	
30th "	"	
31st "	"	

[illegible] Lt Colonel
O.C. A.S.C.
1st I. Cavy Division

1247 W 3299 200,000 (E) 8/14 J.B.C. & A. Forms/C. 2118/11.

Instructions regarding War Diaries and Intelligence Summaries are contained in F. S. Regs., Part II. and the Staff Manual respectively. Title pages will be prepared in manuscript.

WAR DIARY
or
INTELLIGENCE SUMMARY

(Erase heading not required.)

Army Form C. 2118.

Hour, Date, Place	Summary of Events and Information	Remarks and references to Appendices
1st August	Division marched to billets in vicinity of FRUGES. Brigades marched independently on three roads. Transport of LUCKNOW Bde & attached Divl Troops marched under my command. ~~[illegible]~~ ~~[illegible]~~. Went round all Brigades in evening.	
2nd Augt	Division marched to billets in vicinity of BRIMEUX, BEAURANVILLE, AUBYN ST VAAST. Saw transport of LUCKNOW Bde off at starting point & then proceeded to starting point of AMBALA Bde at VERCHOCQ. Saw transport of SIALKOTE Bde rejoining LUCKNOW Bde transport later. Visited all Brigades and Div Hd Qrs in the evening.	
3rd "	Division marched to billets S of line ABBEVILLE – BERNAVILLE with centre about ST RIQUIER. Was long march of over 20 miles. Transport of LUCKNOW Bde was unable to reach starting point at LAMBUS at 7 AM owing to [illegible] of 2nd Ind. Cavy Div.	

1247 W 3299 200,000 (E) 8/14 J.B.C. & A. Forms/C. 2118/11.

Instructions regarding War Diaries and Intelligence Summaries are contained in F. S. Regs., Part II. and the Staff Manual respectively. Title pages will be prepared in manuscript.

WAR DIARY
or
INTELLIGENCE SUMMARY
(Erase heading not required.)

Army Form C. 2118.

Hour, Date, Place	Summary of Events and Information	Remarks and references to Appendices
	having been stopped on a steep hill. This caused a delay of an hour & prevented the transport reaching watering place before Brigade caught it up, necessitating halting till Brigade had passed.	
4th Augt	Division marched to billets in vicinity of DORMAT BOUCHON – FLEXICOURT (exclusive) – HALLOY – MONTRELET	
5th "	Routine. Orders recd to use AF 773 for ration strength to be made out by Supply Officers & submitted through S.S.O to AA&QMG for check with field state	
6th "	Routine	
7th "		
8th "	A & Q Batteries RHA with proportion of Div Amm Column moved to join 10th Corps.	

1247 W 3299 200,000 (E) 8/14 J.B.C. & A. Forms/C. 2118/11.

Instructions regarding War Diaries and Intelligence Summaries are contained in F. S. Regs., Part II. and the Staff Manual respectively. Title pages will be prepared in manuscript.

WAR DIARY
or
INTELLIGENCE SUMMARY
(Erase heading not required.)

Army Form C. 2118.

Hour, Date, Place	Summary of Events and Information	Remarks and references to Appendices
9th Aug.	Routine.	
10th "		
11th "	As 2nd I. Cav. Div. (300 men per Regt) was moving to the trenches & the SIALKOTE Bde of 1st I.C. Div. was ordered to go up in support, I visited O.C. A.S.C. 2nd I. C. Div. to arrange details.	
12th "	SIALKOTE Bde left by busses en route to trenches with A Echelon transport & 2 wagons per unit; the latter to form a train to carry rations from Refilling Point at HEDAUVILLE to MARTINSART where ammunition mules were to carry them on to trenches.	
13th "	Routine	
14th "	Visited Refilling Point ~~at~~ near HEDAUVILLE.	

1247 W 3299 200,000 (E) 8/14 J.B.C. & A. Forms/C. 2118/11.

Instructions regarding War Diaries and Intelligence Summaries are contained in F. S. Regs., Part II. and the Staff Manual respectively. Title pages will be prepared in manuscript.

WAR DIARY
or
INTELLIGENCE SUMMARY
(Erase heading not required.)

Army Form C. 2118.

Hour, Date, Place	Summary of Events and Information	Remarks and references to Appendices
15th August	Routine.	
16th "	"	
17th "	Sanction received for following additional establishment to O.C. Divisional A.S.C. 1 Wheeler (a Corporal) 1 Saddler 1 Shoeing & carriage smith 1 Maltese cart } to be driven by one of the Artificers 1 Horse } The personnel is provided for the purpose of carrying out light running repairs to Transport vehicles & harness & it is hoped considerable economy will be effected.	
18th "	Received following decision as regards terms of enlistment. All mechanical special men are enlisted for the duration of the War All men who enlisted for 1 year are bound to serve the additional 12 months.	

1247 W 3299 200,000 (E) 8/14 J.B.C. & A. Forms/C. 2118/11.

Instructions regarding War Diaries and Intelligence Summaries are contained in F. S. Regs., Part II. and the Staff Manual respectively. Title pages will be prepared in manuscript.

WAR DIARY
or
INTELLIGENCE SUMMARY

(Erase heading not required.)

Army Form C. 2118.

Hour, Date, Place	Summary of Events and Information	Remarks and references to Appendices
19th Augt	G.H.Q Ammunition Park arrived at AILLYS. Attached for Administrative purposes to UMBALLA Bde.	
	Strength —	
	Officers 8	
	R. F 488	
	3 Ton Lorries 131	
	Motor Cars 4	
	" Cycles 8	
	Orders received for Capt. Christie to proceed to GHQ Troops Supply Column for training.	
	2nd Lt. Potts A.S.C from 6th Divl. Train to join 1st Divn	
20th "	Received orders for move of LUCKNOW and AMBALLA Brigades to trenches.	
21st "	Routine.	

1247 W 3299 200,000 (E) 8/14 J.B.C. & A. Forms/C. 2118/11.

Army Form C. 2118.

Instructions regarding War Diaries and Intelligence Summaries are contained in F. S. Regs., Part II. and the Staff Manual respectively. Title pages will be prepared in manuscript.

WAR DIARY
or
INTELLIGENCE SUMMARY
(Erase heading not required.)

Hour, Date, Place	Summary of Events and Information	Remarks and references to Appendices
22nd Augt.	Division moved to wood near FORCEVILLE preparatory to moving into trenches Each Brigade was represented by 300 men per Regt. plus 3/5 officers. Led horses & their men were to return to VADENCOURT & after watering etc to march back to billets A Echelon moved with Brigades & 2 GS Wagons per Unit to form a Train Capt. Saunders DSO detailed to command all A Echelon Capt. Wright to command improvised Train. 2 2nd Lt. Potts A.S.C reported arrival	
23rd Augt.	Division moved into trenches Visited ADS&T. Capt. CHRISTIE reported departure.	

1247 W 3299 200,000 (E) 8/14 J.B.C. & A. Forms/C. 2118/11.

Instructions regarding War Diaries and Intelligence Summaries are contained in F. S. Regs., Part II. and the Staff Manual respectively. Title pages will be prepared in manuscript.

WAR DIARY
or
INTELLIGENCE SUMMARY
(Erase heading not required.)

Army Form C. 2118.

Hour, Date, Place	Summary of Events and Information	Remarks and references to Appendices
24th Augt	U Battery RHA & Gun Sec D.A. Column marched to join 5th Division 10th Corps	
25th "	1 Secn D.A. Park left [illegible] 5th Division. Proceeded to MARTINSART & [illegible] Refilling.	
26th "	Interviewed ADS&T to discuss new forms to be introduced in accounting for Supplies. Received instructions that all questions relating to promotion, replacements etc of RHA drivers now attached to Indian Regts as transport drivers, will be dealt with by O.C. 1st I. RHA Bde	
27th "	Routine	
28th "	Lucknow Bde Hd Qrs moved from CANAPLE to BERNELL. 2nd Lt LUPTON A.S.C joined & posted as R.O. Divl Troops	

Instructions regarding War Diaries and Intelligence Summaries are contained in F. S. Regs., Part II. and the Staff Manual respectively. Title pages will be prepared in manuscript.

WAR DIARY
or
INTELLIGENCE SUMMARY
(Erase heading not required.)

Army Form C. 2118.

Hour, Date, Place	Summary of Events and Information	Remarks and references to Appendices
29th Augt	Inspected Divl Hd Qrs transport 2nd Lt Potts of A.S.C left Division to join 2nd Divl Train	
30th 31st	Routine	
	[illegible] Colonel O.C. A.S.C 1st I.C. Divn	

1247 W 3299 200,000 (E) 8/14 J.B.C. & A. Forms/C. 2118/11.

Instructions regarding War Diaries and Intelligence Summaries are contained in F. S. Regs., Part II. and the Staff Manual respectively. Title pages will be prepared in manuscript.

WAR DIARY
or
INTELLIGENCE SUMMARY

(Erase heading not required.)

Army Form C. 2118.

Hour, Date, Place	Summary of Events and Information	Remarks and references to Appendices
1st Sept.	Routine	
2nd "	"	
3rd "	"	
4th "	"	
5th "		
6th "	Inspected transport of AMBALLA Fd Ambulance two vehicles at front.	
7th "	Inspected LUCKNOW Fd Ambulance. Recd orders with reference to disposal of dismounted men in case the Division advances (Each Indian Cavt Regt has 100 dismounted sowars attached) to new Brigade Supply [illegible] reduction in the number of G.S. Wagons attached to Units for carriage of 2 days supplies — special scale British 3.1 lbs & Indians 2 lbs with forage at 9 lbs per diem	

1247 W 3299 200,000 (E) 8/14 J.B.C. & A. Forms/C. 2118/11.

Instructions regarding War Diaries and Intelligence Summaries are contained in F. S. Regs., Part II. and the Staff Manual respectively. Title pages will be prepared in manuscript.

WAR DIARY
or
INTELLIGENCE SUMMARY
(Erase heading not required.)

Army Form C. 2118.

Hour, Date, Place	Summary of Events and Information	Remarks and references to Appendices
	[illegible] Barges will be moved [illegible] 2 Division will load first. Divl Rendezvous for wagons under O.C. ASC ST SAUVEUR. The wagons will halt at LOMPRE & wait till [illegible] 2nd Divn is within ½ an hour of finishing loading – then move on to the Barges. Wagons of both Divisions will move on to the [illegible] at LES ALENCOURT Ferme where further movements will be communicated	
8th Sept	Inspected GHQ Ammunition Park Everything in excellent order.	
9th "	Routine.	
10th "	Reconnoitred the route for the 'Barge Scheme'	
11th "	Orders having been issued to dump a large amount of coal (50 tons a day) for the Division. Selected a dumping ground at LOMPRE at Ry Station & arranged for 50 suits of dungarees for working party of 40 men to be supplied from Echelons & Fd Ambulances.	

Instructions regarding War Diaries and Intelligence Summaries are contained in F. S. Regs., Part II. and the Staff Manual respectively. Title pages will be prepared in manuscript.

WAR DIARY
or
INTELLIGENCE SUMMARY
(Erase heading not required.)

Army Form C. 2118.

Hour, Date, Place	Summary of Events and Information	Remarks and references to Appendices
12th Sept	Routine.	
13th "	Division relieved 2nd Divn in trenches AMBALLA Bde transferred to 2nd Division & MHOW Bde joined 1st Division. S & T Establishment not changed with exception of Bde Transport Officer — Capt Brooke going with AMBALLA Bde & 2nd Lt Price ASC with MHOW Bde The first batch of 50 tons coal arrived at LOMPRE Newspapers now calculated at 1 paper to 10 men.	
14th Sept	Arranged for a dumping place for baggage & Divl. Troops with reference to Barge Scheme. Five men allotted & the ~~Barge~~ Master to take charge.	
15th "	Orders received that men proceeding on leave were not to take ammunition with them.	

Instructions regarding War Diaries and Intelligence Summaries are contained in F. S. Regs., Part II. and the Staff Manual respectively. Title pages will be prepared in manuscript.

WAR DIARY
or
INTELLIGENCE SUMMARY
(Erase heading not required.)

Army Form C. 2118.

Hour, Date, Place	Summary of Events and Information	Remarks and references to Appendices
16th Sept	Routine	
17th "	Demands for Officers to replace sick casualties to be included in weekly "Present & Fit" return as soon as notification has been received from DAG 3rd Echelon through AG GHQ that officer has been evacuated to England.	
18th "	Received one Battalion cart & one horse to complete Div! ASC Hd Qrs	
19th "	Routine.	
20th "	"	
21st "	Noticed that several wheels of GS Wagons required retyring. Addressed Ordnance on the subject — whether this is to be carried out in Corps travelling Workshops.	

1247 W 3299 200,000 (E) 8/14 J.B.C. & A. Forms/C. 2118/11.

Instructions regarding War Diaries and Intelligence Summaries are contained in F. S. Regs., Part II. and the Staff Manual respectively. Title pages will be prepared in manuscript.

WAR DIARY
or
INTELLIGENCE SUMMARY
(Erase heading not required.)

Army Form C. 2118.

Hour, Date, Place	Summary of Events and Information	Remarks and references to Appendices
22nd Sept	Division moving to billets [illegible]	
23rd "	Routine.	
24th "	Railhead & Corps Headquarters moved to DOULENS	
25th "	B Echelon wagons formed into improvised train to be used where roads will not admit of lorries going whole way. Train divided into two Sections (37 GS Wagons in each Section) each Section carrying 1 days iron rations per man, 9 lbs oats per horse & 1 lb grain emergency ration per horse. The wagons were loaded during night of 25/26 at Railhead & parked on side of road with head at HEM cross roads.	
26th "	Organised the train. O.C. ASC to command with one Officer to each Section. Wagons were by [illegible] to Regts & specially numbered to agree with Supply loading tables.	

1247 W 3299 200,000 (E) 8/14 J.B.C. & A. Forms/C. 2118/11.

Instructions regarding War Diaries and Intelligence Summaries are contained in F. S. Regs., Part II. and the Staff Manual respectively. Title pages will be prepared in manuscript.

WAR DIARY
or
INTELLIGENCE SUMMARY

(Erase heading not required.)

Army Form C. 2118.

Hour, Date, Place	Summary of Events and Information	Remarks and references to Appendices
27th Sept	Auxiliary Horse Coy arrived. This Coy is for carriage of Horse rugs. The organisation of the British Cavalry was to have three Squadrons whereas Regts in Indian Cavalry Corps have four squadrons. This will be rectified.	
	<u>Organisation</u>	
	1 Captain ASC Comdg — Capt Anderson	
	1 Subaltern ASC — Lt [illegible]	
	1 WO	
	1 C Sergt Major	
	1 C.QM Sergt	
	3 Corporals	
	75 drivers for vehicles	
	7 " spare horses	
	5 " spare & general duties	
	2 Batmen	

1247 W 3299 200,000 (E) 8/14 J.B.C. & A. Forms/C. 2118/11.

Instructions regarding War Diaries and Intelligence Summaries are contained in F. S. Regs., Part II. and the Staff Manual respectively. Title pages will be prepared in manuscript.

WAR DIARY
or
INTELLIGENCE SUMMARY
(Erase heading not required.)

Army Form C. 2118.

Hour, Date, Place	Summary of Events and Information	Remarks and references to Appendices
	2 Farriers	
	1 Wheeler	
	1 Saddlers	
	<u>Vehicles & horses</u> <u>horses</u>	
	Bicycles 3	
	Wagons (for ammunition) 32 128	
	Wagons (for blankets) 3 12	
	Water carts 1 2	
	Wagons for baggage & supplies 1 4	
	Wagons spare 1 4	
	Spare 14	

1247 W 3299 200,000 (E) 8/14 J.B.C. & A. Forms/C. 2118/11.

Instructions regarding War Diaries and Intelligence Summaries are contained in F. S. Regs., Part II. and the Staff Manual respectively. Title pages will be prepared in manuscript.

WAR DIARY
or
INTELLIGENCE SUMMARY

(Erase heading not required.)

Army Form C. 2118.

Hour, Date, Place	Summary of Events and Information	Remarks and references to Appendices
28th Sept	Visited Ambulance Horse Coy & arranged for it to billet at MONTIGNY.	
29th "	~~Inspected B Echelon Mhow Bde~~ [partly legible strike-through] Routine	
30	Inspected B. Echelon Mhow Bde	
	[illegible] Lt Colonel O.C. A.S.C 1st Indian Cavy Division	

1247 W 3299 200,000 (E) 8/14 J.B.C. & A. Forms/C. 2118/11.

Army Form C. 2118

WAR DIARY
or
INTELLIGENCE SUMMARY
(Erase heading not required.)

Instructions regarding War Diaries and Intelligence Summaries are contained in F. S. Regs., Part II. and the Staff Manual respectively. Title Pages will be prepared in manuscript.

Place	Date	Hour	Summary of Events and Information	Remarks and references to Appendices
	1st		[illegible]	
	2nd		[illegible]	
	3rd		[illegible]	
	4th		[illegible]	
	5th		[illegible]	

1875 Wt. W593/826 1,000,000 4/15 J.B.C. & A. A.D.S.S./Forms/C. 2118.

Instructions regarding War Diaries and Intelligence Summaries are contained in F. S. Regs., Part II. and the Staff Manual respectively. Title Pages will be prepared in manuscript.

WAR DIARY
or
INTELLIGENCE SUMMARY

(Erase heading not required.)

Army Form C. 2118

Place	Date	Hour	Summary of Events and Information	Remarks and references to Appendices
	6th. [?].10.15		Visited Railhead – 10 ton truck of coal does for whole Corps with supplementary purchases but is rather too little. Inspected 2 more sections of [?] H.T. same condition – ordered to indent for spares & replacements at once, but a little better as regards grease in pipe boxes – those that had grease in their tins or tubs are now depleted. Went to Ord: shed at Railhead & arranged to look to Bde T.O's the balances required of Saddlers & Wheelers tools. These will help to get things right.	
	7th		AA & QMG agrees to cut RHA Batteries 3 bags each (9 bags) on alternate days with DAC (9 bags) to give 4th Sqdn daily extra 9 bags oats. Visited railhead – routine – checked 3316 & 3317 – an excellent system & well worth note for Indian Service practice in lieu of Abstract.	
	8th		Visited Railhead. Inspected 2 Ambulances Tr. best I have seen so far. Spares incomplete and several have unsuitable animals – one 'pair' measured 14.0 & 12.1 hands (mules). Informed ADVS. Harness poorly fitted & breechings utterly unoiled & hanging down to hocks. Brakes want re-adjusting. Inspected 2 sections [?] H Tr – cleaner – indents sent in except [?] Bde.	
	9th		Visited Railhead – Reinforcements arrived – no notice sent to supply service. No carts for their rations to meet them. Sent out one party in lorries at request of RTO no lorries' [?] come to take them to distant billets. Expect rations lost but none traceable yet – Asked SSO's to report. Note AD S&T puts 3316 & 3317 thro' what is equivalent to Indian Audit on the spot & we get an urgent local audit which saves a lot of worry later on. With good Sch: S. Officers of posts [?] in 3316 as fast as they are prepared without much check & see what AD's check brings to light – next to nothing. DADOS complains of heavy indents for carts – no wonder. [?] & DADOS both advocate a spare [?] be stocked to help out cases where perch eye breaks, on limbered GS wagons – 1 per 5 carts. I concurred & hope to get these soon. Insp. A H T Coy carts at Railhead. Animals & carts A1 as seen but men & animals very clumsy & strange to work of course but less so than [?] – Note a return today shows not a single teetotaller in [?]!	

1875 Wt. W593/826 1,000,000 4/15 J.B.C. & A. A.D.S.S./Forms/C. 2118.

Instructions regarding War Diaries and Intelligence Summaries are contained in F. S. Regs., Part II. and the Staff Manual respectively. Title Pages will be prepared in manuscript.

WAR DIARY
or
INTELLIGENCE SUMMARY
(Erase heading not required.)

Army Form C. 2118

Place	Date	Hour	Summary of Events and Information	Remarks and references to Appendices
-------	10.10/15.		Visited Railhead - visited Corps H.Q. & Bᵈᵉ H.Q. portions of Sup: H.T. The equalising bar in majority of cases bent down. Examined this for reason. This point certainly is one to note as a weakness of design due almost certainly to too short a seat, some marks (older ones) have the needful small strip of metal to make all sound but the latest pattern is weak here.	
	11.10/15		Visited Railhead. Routine duties and misc: small arrangements.	
	12.10/15		Brigade areas extended & readjusted with 2nd Bᵈᵉ. [illegible] move and new system worked smoothly. Visited Railhead	
D------	13.10/15		Changed areas completely. Visited Railhead at D-- - a good deal of arrangement necessary to lift coal, to give help to C.I.H. re distributing rations to squadrons. Today I gave some hours to going into a matter of some Admin interest perhaps. Ever since holding appt of Railhead S.T. Officer I have been fairly sure Railhead powers were not used and that the system would be improved greatly by regarding Railhead as a small pool or shunting place always provided the stock was controlled on sound lines. It is clear enough now, for a trial on lines worth trying & I believe would meet B.of C. requirements so far as I can hear or infer them & certainly do troops better & vastly improve executive working.	
	14.10/15		Visited new Railhead & also old railhead. Routine duties. Indian Troops now are to get 3 oz weekly dried fruits in lieu vegetables - from 20.10.15.	
	15.10/15		C.I.H. can not manage to distribute rations from central Regimental dump to Squadrons without H.Q. carts - Heaven knows what they would do if advancing rapidly - but their carts - all other regiments manage well and my diagnosis of the C.I.H. vagaries are that they are temporary.	
	16.10/15		Improved Horse Train suddenly cut down to 1/5 - It has been throughout a most interesting variation from normal [illegible] [illegible] - no more than in its reduction to new condition.	

1875 Wt. W593/826 1,000,000 4/15 J.B.C. & A. A.D.S.S./Forms/C. 2118.

Instructions regarding War Diaries and Intelligence Summaries are contained in F. S. Regs., Part II. and the Staff Manual respectively. Title Pages will be prepared in manuscript.

WAR DIARY
or
INTELLIGENCE SUMMARY
(Erase heading not required.)

Army Form C. 2118

Place	Date	Hour	Summary of Events and Information	Remarks and references to Appendices
D-----	7.10/15		Routine - Visited Railhead - Arranged accounting thro Bdes, DT, 2 Echelon SOs + RSO for shortage grain issues as a "Strategical Issue" to Improvised Horse Train.	
" "	8.10/15		Visited Railhead - Dump at L------ formed + wagons of 3 HT dispersed to units to resume baggage (B Ech) duty	
" "	9.10/15		Major Saunders reported arrival + I put him on as acting SSO - I have now done O/I + SSO for over 2 weeks + must instruct the new offg. officer for a fortnight or so. The D^n is shown on lists with O/Cs appointment vacant. Sgt Sturdy S. T C appointed 2nd Lt Suffolk Regt.	
	20.10/15		Took Offg SSO to Railhead. saw A D S + T + AA + QMG + G H Q there. O/C DSC is arranging billets at new R.H^d	
	21.10/15		Visited Railhead with off SSO. Arranged move details there. Visited O/C 2nd L re Tr spares + indents. Arranged inspection of Regtl Tr with him. Have seen all Tr in driblets by wayside but not as a whole in any unit. No cart in the D^n is complete yet and some 20 carts or so discarded + are getting attention very seriously. Inspr Ord. Machinery is going round D^n steadily + Ord are getting up spares much better.	
	22.10/15		Moved today to L. Q------ area. Truck was hired for coal + nothing abandoned - BSO's managed smoothly. Marched with B Ech D H Q + saw [illegible] Bde B Ech: passing a point also Lucknow Bde Tr at H----- P^t Xing where shunting delayed whole Bde + a B Y R H A 3/4 hour. Moral the tabs of points when arranging marches over level crossing the times of shuntings + passing trains is important. Dismounted men [we have 600 now to have 300 more = 100 per Regt] moved in 2 marches + bivouac at M-------- one night. This composite party was fed smoothly by a simple arrangement in spite of their involving one day's ration of ration strengths in nearly every unit in the D^n	

1875 Wt. W593/826 1,000,000 4/15 J.B.C. & A. A.D.S.S./Forms/C. 2118.

Army Form C. 2118

Instructions regarding War Diaries and Intelligence Summaries are contained in F. S. Regs., Part II. and the Staff Manual respectively. Title Pages will be prepared in manuscript.

WAR DIARY
or
INTELLIGENCE SUMMARY
(Erase heading not required.)

Place	Date	Hour	Summary of Events and Information	Remarks and references to Appendices
------	23.10 / 15		Got the coal distribution arrangements working on permanent method from Railhead. 16 carts of D H T Coy [illegible] 16 lorries by undertaking ration deliveries to units close by – 8 lorries per diem distribute 10 tons of coal. Felt somewhat struck by the economy possible if lorries were used more & horses worked instead of being exercised. Variations from system however rarely prove economical & efficient & this small experiment will show what can be done,	
– „ –	24.10 / 15		Visited Railhead. Dump will be cleared tomorrow I hope. Steps to be taken re Rugs [illegible] – H.M. the King's review for tomorrow postponed to 29th.	
– „ –	25.10 / 15		SSO visited Railhead and started arranging coal fatigue of Naikars under S.S. Harvey STC. Reported to A A & Q M G that L & M Bdes declined to give up 13 Ech carts for Emergency Rations. He issued orders for them to do so forthwith. The art of dealing with Silladar Cav. in connection with S & T matters is a separate branch of military study	
– „ –	26.10 / 15		SSO visited Railhead & settled the Naikar fatigue party down. Adjt went to C--- F--- L A H T Coy who had moved there on 24th – they furnished duty carts quite steadily throughout the past week & worked very hard in vile weather & poor billets. Traffic map called for today. It is curious to note that nowadays the highly trained p.s.c staff officer does not undertake reconnaissance – he is the critic of the efforts of Ty 2nd Lts. 1 Cy who do useful maps & reconnaissances as To officers of both Bde & M T [illegible]. The Staff officer as we know him is really a local – irresponsible – director of executive work which odd jobs have to be thrown [illegible] does not undertake technical staff work. It is a pity the system of staff attachés for the big staff work is not adopted – it would [illegible] instruct & practice young officers & give me a taste for technical staff work & prevent odd jobs being flung at units on service.	
	27.10.15		Capt Wright STC BTO L Bde evacuated sick. SSO visited Railhead. Hydrophobia in this village – 2 cases of mad dogs yesterday. Routine duties	
	28.10 / 15		SSO visited Railhead. Studied equipment of an Inf. Bde Train. A Cav Bde can produce equip ½ an Inf Bde very rapidly if they can find caretakers for their horses rendered surplus. Routine duties	

1875 Wt. W593/826 1,000,000 4/15 J.B.C. & A. A.D.S.S./Forms/C. 2118.

Instructions regarding War Diaries and Intelligence Summaries are contained in F. S. Regs., Part II. and the Staff Manual respectively. Title Pages will be prepared in manuscript.

WAR DIARY
or
INTELLIGENCE SUMMARY

(Erase heading not required.)

Army Form C. 2118

Place	Date	Hour	Summary of Events and Information	Remarks and references to Appendices
L. Q.	29.10/15		Captain Brunker absent - sick in England. After some consideration decided to put up facts of this case. A very hard case indeed & he should not be here at all. A good man rendered useless by bad health & extraordinarily hard luck in private matters - If higher authorities can put it right they will doubtless do so. H.M. The King's inspection was called - some slight accident rumoured. SSO visited Railhead. Routine duties & inspected Tr. animals & carts in my charge. Shoeing smiths are inadequate & evidently scarce.	
	30.10/15		SSO visited Railhead. Routine duties. Sports Committee, instituted.	
	31.10/15		SSO visited Railhead. Routine duties. Traffic maps in - very amateurish so got some simple improvement put in. The want of finish in technique of staff work is illustrated here - not a hint as to whether sectional maps should be joined up to make a map of our area or should be sent in separately - [illegible] result is unnecessary labour somewhere as all maps are in duplicate. The opinions on the durability of French roads are those of [illegible] - the condition varies in most unlikely area so do the opinions.	

H. M. Young Major
O.C. A.S.C. 1st Indian Cavalry Division

1875 Wt. W593/826 1,000,000 4/15 J.B.C. & A. A.D.S.S./Forms/C. 2118.

Instructions regarding War Diaries and Intelligence Summaries are contained in F. S. Regs., Part II. and the Staff Manual respectively. Title pages will be prepared in manuscript.

WAR DIARY
or
INTELLIGENCE SUMMARY.
(Erase heading not required.)

Army Form C. 2118.

Place	Date	Hour	Summary of Events and Information	Remarks and references to Appendices
	1.11.15		Visited Railhead. Saw A.D.S.T about Capt B. Official report leave till 7.11.15. Personally aware he is not likely to return for some weeks. Feel it is my duty to help render this sort of thing impossible + put in a report of the facts for Dir to forward if they so desire.	
	2.11.15		O/C inspected A H T Coy - quite fair turn out in pouring rain - almost complete in spares + gear. Harness nearly all fitted. Carts mostly good as new. Neat device for roller scotch but no possible with latest wheels (with caps). New unit much used since formed. Creditable to O/C. S S O visited railhead - 5 tons coal arrived at Dump.	
	3.11.15		S S O visited R'h'd. O/C inspected Tr of C.I.H. - barely 'tolerable' - Actions taken on spot. Few accessories no tins. Boards Carts suffer from want of paint - Ord: say none at Base. Harness not badly fitted, old bronzed bits have not had the bars cleaned Regt T.O. very keen to learn. B.T.O. lethargic I fear.	
	4.11.15		S.S.O. visited R'h'd. O/C inspected Tr of I. Drgns - Tr worse than C I H - 5 wheels to be changed, two [illegible] boards, little grease in tins accessories + spares still wanting. Bits fairly clean. Harness poorly fitted. Brakes defective. Saw A A + Q M G about Lt Newington's case. Great pity to worry a Ty officer who has apparently acted soundly + properly but DA + QM G sent case to Bde + ignored O/C A S C [Indian system but not Home system] + Bde Major brow beat the young officer verbally + gave him not even a glimpse of the papers - I am glad G O C has taken it into his own hands - Poor luck for a man who chucks up his work on a Singapore estate to join the show + did ditto in S. Africa.	
	[illegible]		Completed 1 month in work as O/C A.S.C. - appointment not yet made pukka -	
	5.11.15		S S O visited Railhead. O/C inspected Transport of 2nd L + B H Q of Mhow Bde - Better than rest of the Bde - B H Q carts not so satisfactory as 2nd L. where C O was present with R T O at inspection.	
	6.11.15		S.S.O. visited Railhead. O/C, Routine + office duties, 5 Br Clerks arrived. [illegible] of move to Tr. Head officially no A S C drivers available at Base.	
	7.11.15		Notice received that Xmas presents are to be promptly cleared from Railhead. Informed S S O of my ideas as to how to use coal dump area for a gifts godown. S S O visited Railhead - Routine duties	
	8.11.15		S.S.O. visited Railhead - B T O's assembled + O/C discussed various small matters.	

2353 Wt. W2544/1454 700,000 5/15 D. D. & L. A.D.S.S./Forms/C. 2118.

Army Form C. 2118.

Instructions regarding War Diaries and Intelligence Summaries are contained in F. S. Regs., Part II. and the Staff Manual respectively. Title pages will be prepared in manuscript.

WAR DIARY
or
INTELLIGENCE SUMMARY.
(Erase heading not required.)

Place	Date	Hour	Summary of Events and Information	Remarks and references to Appendices
Le Q------	9/11/15		Interviewed G.O.C. 0n re Capt Nookes application. S.S.O. visited Railhead. Routine duties + office work.	
	10.11.15		S.S.O. visited Railhead. O/C inspected 17th Lancers Tr. – very good condition and decidedly creditable – The old story young officer 'hazin' – experienced Q.M. in background till questions asked – Too often sneered at the amateur way we work out admin: branches. In peace a Transport or Supply course is avoided + on service Regtl T.O. is changed as quickly as the incumbent can get out of it + the Q.M.s job is not sought after. The consequence is worry on service etc.	
	11.11.15		S.S.O. visited Railhead. O/C inspected Tr. of 6th Cav. Q.B.Y. Sialkote B. H.Q. Fair except one cart of Q.B.Y. This Bde seems to be better than the Mhow Bde all through. The generality of the Tr seems barely satisfactory + looks bad because the Ordnance do not give us paint enough either to keep up a decent appearance or what is far worse preserve the woodwork	
	12.11.15		O/C inspected transport 19th Lancers. S.S.O. visited Railhead. arranged with Inspector ordnance machinery to have cart of Q battery and cart and water cart of 19th Lancers repaired. Went to Metigny to investigate damages done by lorries of Supply Column. No compensation was required. Received circular letter from Director of Supplies bringing to notice that some receipt requisitioning notes misissued were embraced and warning me against these cases. Temporary Lt E. McElliot ASC arrived was posted to Sirhind Brigade as B.T.O.	
	13.11.15		GOC Division inspected Ambala Horse Transport company. He considered there was some improvement since his former inspection in October. Staff Sergeant Austin ASC Supply Column was accepted for commission in the RGA and ordered to proceed to the War Office to report to M.T.3. Sgt Brewster S&TC arrived and was posted to Mhow Brigade	
	14.11.15		S.S.O. went to Railhead	

2353 Wt. W2544/1454 700,000 5/15 D. D. & L. A.D.S.S./Forms/C. 2118.

Instructions regarding War Diaries and Intelligence Summaries are contained in F. S. Regs., Part II. and the Staff Manual respectively. Title pages will be prepared in manuscript.

WAR DIARY

or

INTELLIGENCE SUMMARY.

(Erase heading not required.)

Army Form C. 2118.

Place	Date	Hour	Summary of Events and Information	Remarks and references to Appendices
	15.11.15		Major Saunders S&TC acting for OC ASC went to Corps HdQrs. DAQMG Indian Cavalry Corps discussed matter concerning SECRET scheme of dismounted division and arranged with OCS Divisional Supply Column to form a dismounted Supply Column in two echelons on Cavalry principles. Details etc discussed and arranged. Submitted proposals for promotion of IARO S&T Corps officers with a view to taking up vacancies of BSOs as they might occur.	
	16.11.15		S.S.O. went to Railhead. Capt A S J Wright S&TC returned to duty from hospital & posted BSO [illegible] Horse Brigade vice Captain Brunker struck off strength (sick). Confidential letter from Director of Supplies received re employment of French Interpreters being used as purchasing officers being forbidden. Circulated to BSOs & S.O. D.T. also OC Supply Column & Park (acknowledged).	
	17.11.15		SSO went to Railhead. The Supply Column moved to billets in Airaines. This was done because being horse sickness there it could not be used for any unit with horses. Arranged for move of horse rugs for those units moving. Whale oil to be issued only to Indian troops for the trenches. Anti-frost grease being supplied to British Troops only.	
	18.11.15		Lucknow Brigade and a portion of Sialkot Brigade moved billets the object being to close up the Division into a smaller area. The DD S&T called for confidential reports on the Indian Clerks. We were informed that we were asking for too much coal, the scale of 1½ lbs per man plus 50 lbs for fireplaces was not to be exceeded. Coal was not to be issued in lieu of wood. Visited OC ASC 2nd Indian Cav Dn at OISEMENT to settle some details in the Dismounted Division Scheme. S.S.O had a conference with BSOs on the same subject. Capt J Sealy Bell reported his arrival, asked AA & QMG for orders as to disposal	

2353 Wt. W2541/1454 700,000 5/15 D. D. & L. A.D.S.S./Forms/C. 2118.

Instructions regarding War Diaries and Intelligence Summaries are contained in F. S. Regs., Part II. and the Staff Manual respectively. Title pages will be prepared in manuscript.

WAR DIARY
or
INTELLIGENCE SUMMARY.
(Erase heading not required.)

Army Form C. 2118.

Place	Date	Hour	Summary of Events and Information	Remarks and references to Appendices
	18.11.15		(Continued) Divisional order published that 100 men (dismounted) per regiment should keep one days ordinary rations in hand in case of a move to be turned over. Letter received from ADST to reduce demands for bran for a few days owing to scarcity at the base.	
	19.11.15		SSO went to railhead oat and bread sacks to be returned to railhead for return to the base.	
	20.11.15		Took Capt Noakes and Capt Sealy Bell to interview ASC Division. Cav. Horse Tr Company moved from METIGNY to LE QUESNOY. O Battery RHA moved from Bettencourt to Metigny. Letter received from ADST informing special kitchen coal arriving 22nd. Report after a weeks trial required whether suitable for all purposes. Warned not to fold up motor car hoods when wet orders issued.	
	21.11.15		Received orders for Major M de B Scott ASC commanding Ammunition Park to proceed to THIENNES to take over command of the Meerut Supply Column	
	22.11.15		Lt and Temporary Captain HJM Howard ASC takes over command of the Ammunition Park. Orders received that no drivers or gunners of the RA are to be permitted to transfer to Mechanical Transport. Authority in Divisional orders to issue two blankets per man. SSO went to railhead	

2353 Wt. W2544/1454 700,000 5/15 D. D. & L. A.D.S.S./Forms/C. 2118.

Instructions regarding War Diaries and Intelligence Summaries are contained in F. S. Regs., Part II. and the Staff Manual respectively. Title pages will be prepared in manuscript.

WAR DIARY
or
INTELLIGENCE SUMMARY.
(Erase heading not required.)

Army Form C. 2118.

Place	Date	Hour	Summary of Events and Information	Remarks and references to Appendices
~~23~~	23.11.15		G.O.C Corps inspected remounts. S.S.O presided at committee at 12 noon to enquire into a complaint made by an inhabitant of Lequesnoy. Orders received that all S&T Corps returns on personnel in future to be rendered to A.D.S&T I Cav Corps and not to D.D.S&T Indian Contingent. Orders received that no coal is to be purchased locally, all coal will be arranged for with Bruay Mines through the S.S.O. Glycerine is scarce. Received new bus time table for Trench scheme.	
	24.11.15		S.S.O went to railhead. Wheelers and Saddlers detached from Field Ambulances & Brigade H.Qrs have been withdrawn on the reduction of establishment of Field Ambs by 1 saddler and 1 wheeler. The question of farriers is still under consideration. Reply received to letter recommending R.Os of the I.A.R. S&T Corps for promotion to the effect that R.Os need not be of any particular rank, but in the event of vacancies occurring amongst B.S.Os our interests are watched by O.M.C. A.S.C. G.H.Q who will fill vacancies by suitable officers and that our establishment of S&T officers will not be reduced below a workable minimum. Names of R.O may be submitted in due course for rewards for good services.	
	25.11.15		Indian Clerks were despatched to Marseilles in communication with 2nd Ind Cav. Division. 175 lbs cardamoms being sent weekly to railhead (part of a gift from Indian friends) from Havre where they are stored. Report called for by Div H.Q. number of tents required for drying purposes & whether tents are suitable for the purpose. Also whether fuel can be met out of the fuel ration. Circulated to A.S.C units.	

2353 Wt. W2544/1454 700,000 5/15 D. D. & L. A.D.S.S./Forms/C. 2118.

Instructions regarding War Diaries and Intelligence Summaries are contained in F. S. Regs., Part II. and the Staff Manual respectively. Title pages will be prepared in manuscript.

WAR DIARY
or
INTELLIGENCE SUMMARY.

(Erase heading not required.)

Army Form C. 2118.

Place	Date	Hour	Summary of Events and Information	Remarks and references to Appendices
[illegible]	26.11.15		S.S.O. visited Railhead	
	27.11.15		O/C A.S.C. returned last night from leave in U.K. S.S.O. visited Railhead. O/C Routine duties + office work making up past 10 days' arrears [illegible]	
	28.11.15		S.S.O. visited Railhead. O/C routine duties + office work. [illegible] for Railhead rooms rather difficult to arrange owing to shortage of oil [illegible] S.S.O. [illegible] the question.	
	29.11.15		S.S.O. visited Railhead. O/C went to Railhead with the S.S.O. [illegible] regarding [illegible] application [illegible] regards recent orders to Maires of Communes & the [illegible] The result is said to have been [illegible] and is understood at G.H.Q. [illegible] complete [illegible] and [illegible] carts only should be sent to [illegible] found convenient to [illegible] but there is no objection to wood being issued in lieu of coal [illegible] for all purposes [illegible]	
	30.11.15		S.S.O. visited Railhead. O/C Routine duties. O/C D.S.C. [illegible] Lt Col Kennedy joined [illegible] Staff Officer.	

2353 Wt. W2544/1454 700,000 5/15 D. D. & L. A.D.S.S./Forms/C. 2118.

Instructions regarding War Diaries and Intelligence Summaries are contained in F. S. Regs., Part II. and the Staff Manual respectively. Title pages will be prepared in manuscript.

WAR DIARY
or
INTELLIGENCE SUMMARY.
(Erase heading not required.)

Army Form C. 2118.

1914 & 1915

Place	Date	Hour	Summary of Events and Information	Remarks and references to Appendices
L-Q......	1.12.15		SSO visited Railhead. Experimental 2nd qual. coal issued. Extra blanket for Indians (after troops in trenches fully issued) sanctioned - vide [illegible] Order.	
	2.12.15		Visited DS[illegible] with AA & QMG re Routes to be used by lorries. SSO visited Railhead. 3 Wheelers & 3 Saddlers sent to H T Depot Havre - these are the [illegible] [illegible] [illegible] to Cav [illegible] Amb.	
	3.12.15		O/C inspected 29th L Tr after GOC's inspection. Bodily average, harness fits badly, accessories of carts less incomplete than usual. Bde H Q Tr was not any better than the Regt. Carts sounds. [illegible] in satisfactory condition but some suffer owing to harness [illegible] to gall them. Took BTO & RO round for 1½ hours teaching them to observe faults.	
	4.12.15		SSO visited Railhead. O/C ASC assembled BSO's & RO's in office & explained situation regarding local purchase & rates now that Maire's under Fr Mission instructions are taking [illegible] re [illegible] local farm produce [illegible] effect tending to form Communal rings. Prices going up. RO's [illegible] to accept flat ([illegible]) rates and this O/C directed them to avoid pointing out that this is [illegible] it must result in [illegible] rates - [illegible] bargains direct with producers, giving trade to those who accept low rates & withholding trade from the less reasonable & showing producers that we can get produce at reasonable rates will nearly always result in far better rates & in [illegible] or checking [illegible] rates. The average rates the crux & this we have always & will with work always keep below any flat rates. The RO's are constantly still [illegible] owing to the [illegible] [illegible] Dept challenging rates but never expressing appreciation - they have done extraordinary good clever work & never get a word of appreciation except from me. Mentioned this to ADS&T who will I understand keep this in mind. The 'Investigation' title might be 'Statistical' instead perhaps.	
	5.12.15		SSO visited Railhead. Orders received to keep a large portion of our roads clear of traffic for an Inf Div. This point is noted as an instance of short notice (orders on 5th for 5th 6th & 7th [illegible]) and the necessity for looking out for this class of block in our system. In this case no trouble experienced.	

Army Form C. 2118.

WAR DIARY
or
INTELLIGENCE SUMMARY.
(*Erase heading not required.*)

Instructions regarding War Diaries and Intelligence Summaries are contained in F. S. Regs., Part II. and the Staff Manual respectively. Title pages will be prepared in manuscript.

Place	Date	Hour	Summary of Events and Information	Remarks and references to Appendices
as before	6.12.15		SSO visited Railhead. The batteries are to move to outside formation, Iron rations to be dumped. DSC warned so far as possible about Batteries, DAC & S.A.P. This sort of transfer of units necessarily exemplifies what I believe to be our principal weak point in Regs & instructions — No where exists clear orders as to what to do when a unit is shifted from one formation to another — or any other "process" — Everybody's idea is that this sort of process is [illegible] — For instance "2 Batteries to be transferred to — Army" is what we hear. No one knows if a proportion of DAC & DAP & DSC are to be detached — to which railhead (or railheads) whether on the Inf. or Cav system. This process unearthed the fact last time that some Corps & Army Staffs hand this over to R.A. authorities en bloc & latter's staff have no Q officer or Q knowledge & forget that Batteries have to be fed (so to speak). Our regs are in books such that all services (& staff) concerned are [illegible] & look to different books & thus tend to isolate action — no where can one find all that has to be done e.g. when transferring a unit, entraining a unit, embarking a unit, adding to the establ. of a unit, detaching part of a unit; so that the staff & all concerned can see how all branches & depts work in with one another & with the units concerned. Not all those concerned are experienced staffs & [illegible] officers [illegible] [illegible] memoirs or note books of compiled regulations & orders. This my opinion is strengthened by experience.	
— " —	7.12.15		SSO visited Railhead: Emergency Iron rations dumped in BSSO's charge. BTO's returned cash to units. Shakarpara emergency rusks for Indians — sample being kept by me — completed 6 months in ordinary flap lid tin — still quite good. O/C A B4 started out of D area.	
	8.12.15		SSO Railhead. Bran sacks to be returned to Base. Tents for drying purposes approved 15lbs straw to cover bonnets of lorries — anti frost protection.	
	9.12.15		SSO at Railhead. Inspected HDG's Tr — fairly good. same points as in previous units — about average of British Regts —	

2353 Wt. W2544/1454 700,000 5/15 D. D. & L. A.D.S.S./Forms/C. 2118.

Instructions regarding War Diaries and Intelligence Summaries are contained in F. S. Regs., Part II. and the Staff Manual respectively. Title pages will be prepared in manuscript.

WAR DIARY
or
INTELLIGENCE SUMMARY.
(Erase heading not required.)

Army Form C. 2118.

Place	Date	Hour	Summary of Events and Information	Remarks and references to Appendices
	10.12.15		SSO + O/C attended Tr. Warfare Scheme Conference – Considerable amount of Q work allotted to O/C verbally. Visited the trench plot on fields + framed notes on O/C's portion. Postponed Tr inspection.	
	11.12.15		36th J. Horse Tr inspected – saddlery virtually not fitted at all – improperly put on animals. Hoofs worst in Dr + carts uncared for, animals show rubs + galls – a very poor show. Warned R.T.O. + B.T.O. very seriously + promised to inspect this lot again!	
	12.12.15		A H T Coy distributed to Bdes + DT – SSO visited Railhead. Carts move to take kits to new area. Lt KINGSELL arrived, posted him to Lucknow to replace Lt ELIOT left for B.S. Depot. SSO at Railhead	
	13.12.15		AHT Coy carts returned from new area. SSO visited Railhead.	
	14.12.15		Official orders to move to new area received with Admin Instrns + billets. Dismounted men moved – 1 Bde by Rail + rest by lorries. SSO went to Railhead + I accompanied him to see A.D.S.+T. + inspect.	
	15.12.15		S.S.O. visited railhead, sent on SO + RO DT to new area – wood is the special difficulty + is said to be very scarce. It seems to be a coal using area along the Railways + forests exist only outside the area.	
	16.12.15		Marched to OISEMENT with D.H.Q. Tr – thence independently watching various units Tr. Saw 1 Regt, 1 Amb + 2 DT units. Note When civilian hired Tr is used it should move last. Same note as usual about overloading but it was not bad in any instance this time.	
	17.12.15		The new Railhead is inconvenient but must be made to do – long run for lorries tho' 2nd Dn to 1st Dn. All supplies reported scarce + farmers ringed by Maires. Wood v. scarce, potatoes exhausted (?) by Abbeville, fodder [illegible] farmers &c – old story – probably has some foundation but stuff will appear in time. Coal dump at CHEPY very convenient + the balance from Long [illegible] shifted [illegible]!	

2353 Wt. W2544/1454 700,000 5/15 D. D. & L. A.D.S.S./Forms/C. 2118.

WAR DIARY
or
INTELLIGENCE SUMMARY.

(Erase heading not required.)

Army Form C. 2118.

Instructions regarding War Diaries and Intelligence Summaries are contained in F. S. Regs., Part II. and the Staff Manual respectively. Title pages will be prepared in manuscript.

Place	Date	Hour	Summary of Events and Information	Remarks and references to Appendices
	18.12.15		Railhead visited by SSO. – at BLAGNY – there are Rly technical objections to this Railhead & we have Road approach & traffic objections & also want more space & yard facilities. Local supplies already begin to ease off considerably wood being the main anxiety. Inspected H.Q. Tr. billets & stabling – quite satisfactory.	
	19.12.15		SSO visited Railhead & arranged re coal at CHEPY where we are having a dump & the A.H.T. Coy for distribution to Bdes. I mean to use this dump in several ways & it is a decided convenience when not on the move to have a local central dump. It occurred to me some time ago that Railheads are not developed as 'conveniences' for field formations enough & the utility of the dump has tended to harden this opinion – I think mobility & many of the less obvious 'aids to efficiency' might be enhanced if the Railhead were studied with a view to find out if – all things considered – it could not be made more generally useful to field formations. Some principles rules or practised customs are a shade too rigidly restrictive as seen from my point of view – but this aspect is limited & there are factors of which I can only surmise the importance. There seems scope for study in this connection.	
	20.12.15		SSO ~~visited~~ Railhead & arranged with Capt Noake re wood supply in his absence – Capt N. will act as SSO. DA & QMG Col R.C.W. inspected Sialkote Bde Tr. O/C attended. All satisfactory except S. Cav F Amb which had a peculiar series of misfortunes – all officers under arrest – NCO sick – new O.C. – Their Tr was not bad but harness was badly put on by new drivers & carts not smart – all serviceable but I shall shift the NCO who is not at all first class.	
	21.12.15		SSO visited Railhead at GAMACHES – better Railhead, better traffic roads to it from all billets but road cause anxiety. Sides there & under soil out, spongey and undrained. Interviews Austin III & Harvey Sgt DSC views to Conseils. Lucknow Bde inspected by DA & QMG – all good, Mules hoofs as in previous Bde noted on as imperfect – a bad point in the mules all thro'. A showy & sound – tendency to deal with area questions at Corps H.Q. is noticeable – result is we get good circulars for information. Reports on resources in forages, billets, traffic maps, roads & repairs, re called for.	
	22.12.15		SSO went on leave. Railhead not visited as O/C attended inspection of Tr of Mhow Bde by DA & QMG, & Capt Noake is busy with wood supply by M. Cos P.K. (H.T.) & Aux H.T. Coy from S. Riquier to CHEPY – 38th C.I. Horse worst Regt – Inniskilling Dgns a bit better. 2nd L decidedly improved – 38th C.I.H. had improved well considering time available since I saw them last but they need more work & I told them clearly that they should give a lot of work to their Tr.	
	23.12.15		SSO (acty) visited Railhead. Wood supply flowing in well generally & CHEPY dump will have a fair reserve soon. Tr inspection of D Tr. Transport postponed. I arranged to see 40 Sqdns in a few days time. They are good as seen passing by but I have not seen their technical vehicles at close quarters.	

Instructions regarding War Diaries and Intelligence Summaries are contained in F. S. Regs., Part II. and the Staff Manual respectively. Title pages will be prepared in manuscript.

WAR DIARY
or
INTELLIGENCE SUMMARY.
(Erase heading not required.)

Army Form C. 2118.

Place	Date	Hour	Summary of Events and Information	Remarks and references to Appendices
	24.12.15		SSO (actg) visited Railhead. Today we dumped rations deliverable tomorrow to give BSC an easy Xmas day. Dumped the Iron Rations (2 days special) at CHEPY coal & wood dump. This puts all but 5 loads near the AHT Coy who can spare 9 carts for them & not far from DHQ whence 5 more must be detailed for the balance. These rations are such a resource that tho a nuisance in some ways I am inclined to suggest that Cav: should have these rations & carts for them as a matter of fixed organisation. The fact governing this case seems to me to be that they give cavalry say two days extra radius as regards rations & so far as I can work it out rations for men in the spring (fodder growing season) is the limiting factor for Cavalry. Even in this fertile populated land I doubt Cav finding any edibles for men over the French line for miles during operations – in the growing season before the enemy can crop or burn grass the horses will get a bite anywhere.	
	25.12.15		Xmas Day. Not much in office – Men had, in all units, a Xmas dinner and gifts were numerous & handsome.	
	26.12.15		SSO (actg) visited Railhead. 41 horses of DHQ & ASC HQ mallened. WO letter arrived urging use of HT instead of lorries as possible. We have steadily done this to max possible & are using 30–50 Mounted Res Park carts for wood as well as all our HT. It is a sound thing & the WO letter from its wording appears to be based on Inf: practice so it is probably a matter largely for us to regard as confirmation of our practice rather than as a fresh suggestion. I am somewhat inclined to note that the higher authorities would make us less anxious & worried if whenever possible the lesser offices could be given a hint as to what applies to the latter quâ orders & what applies quâ information – The Corps HQ & probably GHQ have a pretty accurate notion as to the Divs where HT is used to lessen expenditure, where purchasing is closely economical, where functions severally are well controlled & these often get letters which are puzzling unless one assumes that other Divs need a special order – also some men who are nervous think they are being strafed & do worry in a futile way where worry is useless & leave aside the lines where worry would bear good fruit. I have had to write yards of reports & statements & visit ADS&T & confer & talk for hours about petty details of past weeks so as to provide half a dozen offices with detailed proof that we took the obvious line of using H.T. to economise in petrol &c – where our main – & larger – aim was to preserve the M.T. in tip top condition by keeping max number of lorries in the repair & overhauling workshop & unused since last visit there to it would express our idea better perhaps if the aim were described as "to keep our lorries constantly available for overhaul & repairs & adjustments to the maximum & to reduce chances of any being inefficient at a critical moment to the min". It is the commonly accepted axiom for M.T. applied to service conditions & nothing peculiar.	
	27.12.15		SSO (actg) visited Railhead. Inquiry as to whether BSO's can properly arrange to get Regts to draw Rations at B. HQ on HT. This involves the drawback of [illegible] handling & expense of rations but would save some road & lorry wear in a few cases if purchasing officers & units can release the necessary carts in these few cases. I doubt its expediency.	

2353. Wt. W2541/1454. 700,000 5/15. D. D. & L. A.D.S.S./Forms/C. 2118.

Instructions regarding War Diaries and Intelligence Summaries are contained in F. S. Regs., Part II. and the Staff Manual respectively. Title pages will be prepared in manuscript.

WAR DIARY
or
INTELLIGENCE SUMMARY.
(Erase heading not required.)

Army Form C. 2118.

Place	Date	Hour	Summary of Events and Information	Remarks and references to Appendices
	28.12.15		D.A.G. Lt Holmes (to Lapse) to become S.O. Corps Tr vice Capt Sampson S&TC (dec) SSO (actg) visited Railhead. New periodical — Weekly Return to ADS&T of arrivals of Coal trucks. These returns are multiplying very fast & becoming more & more detailed. It is a point to note whether a regular stock a/c showing receipts issues & balances should not be designed as the basis of requirements & that orders should be confined to indicating what columns or lines on it may be left blank or used for approximations. Higher authorities are always aware of what they want but the executive worry themselves with the doubts which inevitably arise — Our wood & coal weekly return for instance has (a) a daily consumption figure (b) in next col[n] a weekly consumption figure — then comes a pair of columns "amts actually received" — by whom is not stated — is it by units for consumption or by Bdes for distribution or by the D[n] as a whole — then there comes a col[n] for balances on hand at the end of the week — It is in fact an abstract from a regular stock a/c — it purports to me to be an admin: report — but it is open to suspicion that it will be subjected to audit in connection with the weekly purchase statement &c where the whole of the same facts are submitted in another form — are we going to be called on to dig out reconciliation statements between these two a/c's. The expediency of sinking our executive convenience to the accounts instead of the a/c to the best executive method is in question. In my humble opinion the next figure that has to be evolved it may be best to start stock a/c with Receipts so that it can be audited later & entries connected up accurately — more accurately than fact & based on estimated weights — We don't do much weighing of wood & coal as everyone can judge it near enough to concern in practical transactions — This is not due to aversion from accuracy but to want of weighing machines & transport to carry such gear. Trench returns conference.	
	29.12.15		SSO returned from leave & Capt Noakes to Sialkote Bde, Lt H R Howard MC to 7.1.16. Saddler Dickie Lucknow Bde & 3 Indian car drivers rec'd by ADMS. Naik Pandu, Deolal, De Souza.	
	30.12.15		Lt Holmes reported Dep & took home 9 batman as temp'y measure. SSO visited Railhead.	
	31.12.15		SSO visited Railhead. We are to report how much potatoes exist in our area after allowing "sufficient" for the inhabitants — Seeing that we pay only 60–75% of our next door neighbours & that our area is a fair sized country with sea, rail, river, canal & road communications & that the inhabitants import much of this supply our conclusion on this point must be inconclusive.	
			H M Young	

2353 Wt. W2544/1454 700,000 5/15 D. D. & L. A.D.S.S./Forms/C. 2118.

Instructions regarding War Diaries and Intelligence Summaries are contained in F. S. Regs., Part II. and the Staff Manual respectively. Title pages will be prepared in manuscript.

WAR DIARY
or
INTELLIGENCE SUMMARY.
(Erase heading not required.)

Army Form C. 2118.

Place	Date	Hour	Summary of Events and Information	Remarks and references to Appendices
–––	1.1.16		S.S.O. visited Railhead. 2 Lt. [illegible] join D^n in lieu of Lt H. [illegible] – from Rouen.	
	2.1.16		S.S.O. visited Railhead. Shifting road metal from quarry to road side (200 carts x trips) + spreading it. (1 ½ Sqdn + 24 [illegible]) [illegible] – 6 carts did 4 trips each between 9 a.m. + 3 p.m. Am a little anxious about the roads if weather becomes bad.	
	3.1.16		[illegible] A.S.C. visited railhead + informed A.D.S.T. regarding unsuitability of [illegible] (crushing). There is a minute [illegible] in the S^y system illustrated by this supply but it affects all unrestricted supplies of the "as required" variety. [illegible] stocks are maintained at Railhead [illegible] A.D.S.T. presses for exact figures for one consignment of supplies for week – (c) [illegible] experts (Med) can not estimate what would be required [illegible] without waste + anyway want it immediately – always. The only economic solution of this difficulty is a small stock at Railhead – or an extra cart or small stock with Bde S.O's. I favour the latter solution because in some instances the stuff is required at once to be efficacious – there are drawbacks connected with Railhead stocks here – where we do not control the Rep + are requested to avoid dumps in [illegible] yards. 1 ½ tons per Bde would solve the whole set of difficulties – which are petty, recurrent, constant, irritating + slightly different. These are difficult to explain + to sum up but after a years continuous experience I think a solution should be decided on + allowing for varied exigencies, differences of local conditions &c in my opinion the cart [illegible] is the most economical [illegible] think of + also the best – the main objection is the possibility of that vehicle being appropriated for other uses – [illegible]!	
	4.1.16		S.S.O. visited Railhead. O/C inspected wood cutting parties – Birch + plane stool wood is being cut. [illegible] It is worth while for S.O. to know [illegible] about f.s. wood supply as this locally acquired supply is a difficult one [illegible] knowledge makes for the advantage of the troops + full advantage of local resources. [illegible] be clipped.	
	5.1.16		S.S.O. – Railhead. O/C inspected H.T. of [illegible] Cav F^d Amb. Decidedly above average – water cart [illegible] [illegible] The H.Q. [illegible] G.S. Wagons NOT be used for road metal carting. [illegible] work is noticeable in this Tr. – [illegible]	
	6.1.16		S.S.O. – Railhead. O/C inspected vehicles of Amb^ce Col. – a few points to improve – notably good. [illegible] [illegible] R.A. officers + N.C.Os &c + the condition of animals harness + vehicles is proportionately good. [illegible] the serious necessity for sacrificing much in peace time to teach all ranks the importance of [illegible] standard – instructed men make such a vast difference. the Transport [illegible]	

2353 Wt. W2544/1454 700,000 5/15 D. D. & L. A.D.S.S./Forms/C. 2118.

Instructions regarding War Diaries and Intelligence Summaries are contained in F. S. Regs., Part II. and the Staff Manual respectively. Title pages will be prepared in manuscript.

WAR DIARY
or
INTELLIGENCE SUMMARY.
(Erase heading not required.)

Army Form C. 2118.

Place	Date	Hour	Summary of Events and Information	Remarks and references to Appendices
	7.1.16		SSO Railhead. O/C ASC, went with SSO & saw AD S&T regarding (a) reduction of railhead supply of hay from 10 to 6 lbs and as regards (b) making up a reserve. To take effect on 12th. The official orders not yet out. Matter decidedly serious however. Resources very small in this area. French are buying ½ hay crop. Wheat & hay short	
	8.1.16		Drafted orders regarding fodder supply – maintain as near 12 lbs as possible but reduce units to say up to say 2 lbs per diem. Lay in 120 lbs per horse of local produce. Consume this reserve saving baled stuff instead of loose fodder which dump at central point near Railhead. Purchases hard to get quickly & enough. SSO visited Railhead	
	9.1.16		SSO visited Railhead – O/C accompanied. 6 lbs hay came up in lieu of 10 today instead of 12th inst. Fodder is being bought but there is not much to spare as this is a factory area to S. – on N. there is more farming. It will be a very near thing. AD S&T says our ideas are sound & he approves. Visited ADOS who states purchases available but I expect to have to wait a week or more. Saw AA & QMG regarding road traffic &c. O/C ASC has already conformed with my approval to O/C DT Sqdns recommendations – Roads are becoming a serious matter as regards deliveries to units billets but are A I for movements.	
	10.1.16		SSO & O/C ASC visited Railhead. O/C saw AD S&T with 2nd in O/C ASC present. AA+QMG (acting DA) present. The question of 'Thawing' roads discussed. Res Park are going to give us 46 carts. No MT traffic allowed – 3 days reserve of fodder to be maintained by units. H.T. will be very heavily worked indeed. I fear but for 3 days only. I represented the wood, fodder & vegetable situation & it was agreed that prolongation of 3 days 'thaw' measures would scarcely be expedient. Notice that I shall be required to act as AD S&T was verbally given to me.	

Instructions regarding War Diaries and Intelligence Summaries are contained in F. S. Regs., Part II. and the Staff Manual respectively. Title pages will be prepared in manuscript.

WAR DIARY
or
INTELLIGENCE SUMMARY.
(Erase heading not required.)

Army Form C. 2118.

Place	Date	Hour	Summary of Events and Information	Remarks and references to Appendices
	11.1.16		SSO visited Railhead. Comdr Gale arrived yesterday. Workshops of DSC moved from BEAUCHAMPS to WOINCOURT. Mark 8 GS Wagons of DAC - recommended that these be fitted with 2nd Cl C axles & 2nd Class No 200 wheels. Reduction of fodder from 10 to 6 lbs [by Train] orders & warnings issued.	
	12.1.16		Reduction of fodder took effect today unexpectedly 2 days before named date. SSO & O/C ASC visited Railhead.	
	13.1.16		Motor cars to be overhauled & frames to be inspected fortnightly by O/C DSC. Thaw Scheme received & orders drafted. SSO visited Railhead.	
	14.1.16		Visited AHT Coy: Question of non-inoculated men taken up. Purchasing Rates in Sialkote Bde using -	
	15.1.16		S.S.O. visited Railhead - Routine office duties. Bad mending carts seen - civilian carts do well with our harness.	
	16.1.16		Question of 200 & 200A wheels - AHQ wants 200A wheels till supply is exhausted - Not a matter of great moment as explained but I am inclined to think 200 pattern would have been a sounder decision in the existing circumstances. Speed limit of cars - several reported for exceeding limits. Supply transactions to go to Railhead.	
	17.1.16		O/C ASC left to officiate as ADS&T, Corps HQ. - Thaw Scheme ASC orders issued. Court of enquiry on accident to bicycle of Corps Sig Sqdn & RD DTs car.	

Army Form C. 2118.

Instructions regarding War Diaries and Intelligence Summaries are contained in F. S. Regs., Part II. and the Staff Manual respectively. Title pages will be prepared in manuscript.

WAR DIARY
or
INTELLIGENCE SUMMARY.

(Erase heading not required.)

Place	Date	Hour	Summary of Events and Information	Remarks and references to Appendices
	18.1.16		Lt Col H. Young went to Corps H^d Q^rs to act for ADST. Major Saunders acting as O.C. ASC	
	19.1.16		Temp^y Lt Howard [illegible] Park went to interview DDST 3rd Army reference permanent commission. Captain Wright resumed BSO [illegible] B^de. Capt Pyrah resumed Echelon Supply Officer to S Column. Visited ADST in afternoon.	
	20.1.16		Received circular referring to French delegates visiting our area to investigate condition of [illegible] of [illegible] etc - BSOs [illegible] BTOs hired civilian carts for removing road metal - Total 16 -	
	21.1.16		SSO went to Railhead.	
	22.1.16		Received orders regarding transfer of Capt A.S. [illegible] to 2nd Division as SSO and 2/Lt Partridge to replace vacancy. 2/Lieut [illegible] to take over BSO Sialkot Brigade.	
	23.1.16		The Aux Horse Transport company received 23 reinforcements ASC drivers to complete complement.	
	24.1.16		10% extra tube helmets (gas) sanctioned for instructional purposes. 2nd Lieut Westcott ASC left for GHQ on appointment to flying corps. 2/Lt Canton ASC arrived to replace Lt Westcott.	

2353 Wt. W2544/1454 700,000 5/15 D. D. & L. A.D.S.S./Forms/C. 2118.

Instructions regarding War Diaries and Intelligence Summaries are contained in F. S. Regs., Part II. and the Staff Manual respectively. Title pages will be prepared in manuscript.

WAR DIARY
or
INTELLIGENCE SUMMARY.
(Erase heading not required.)

Army Form C. 2118.

Place	Date	Hour	Summary of Events and Information	Remarks and references to Appendices
	25.1.16.		The establishment for the Butchery at Railhead left for Rouen. Butchery transferred there. Received orders for 2/Lt Canton to proceed No 5 G.H.Q. Ammunition Park and 2nd/Lt James appointed to Divisional Supply Column.	
	26.1.16.		Canadian Cavalry Brigade with Canadian R.H.A. Brigade arrived and is attached to 1st Indian Cav Dn.	
	27.1.16		Report sent to A.D.S.T. of reserves of fodder potatoes and wood on hand. Orders received re dismounted party proceeding to front. S.S.O. arranged for delivery of rations to Canadian Bde.	
	28.1.16		[illegible] of Canadian Bde [illegible] 2 p.m.	
	29.1.16		2/Lt Young rejoined from A.D.S.T. office & Maj. Saunders went on leave to England. Orders issued (incoming) cancelled regarding move of [illegible] Horse. [illegible] Lucknow Bde [illegible] instructions to S.S.O. [illegible] re Dismounted party. Instructions issued to T.S.O. [illegible] re supplies fodder & grain [illegible] transfer of [illegible] from [illegible] to Canadian Cav. [illegible] Telephoned reports to A.D.S.T. (1) re [illegible] supplies [illegible] (2) the [illegible] in the [illegible] GAMACHES [illegible]. Lucknow Bde reports possession of [illegible] lbs fodder per horse.	

Instructions regarding War Diaries and Intelligence Summaries are contained in F. S. Regs., Part II. and the Staff Manual respectively. Title pages will be prepared in manuscript.

WAR DIARY
or
INTELLIGENCE SUMMARY.

(Erase heading not required.)

Army Form C. 2118.

Place	Date	Hour	Summary of Events and Information	Remarks and references to Appendices
"	30.1.16		Visited ADVS at Railhead regarding shortage of Drivers for [illegible]. Also [illegible] Bde [illegible] for fodder. Visited Refilling Point of Canadian Bde and saw their work – [illegible] horses of good type & condition. Saw [illegible]	
"	31.1.16		Made out recommendations for next month for mentions &c. [illegible] Today [illegible] 6 horses per Regt [illegible].	

2353 Wt. W2544/1454 700,000 5/15 D. D. & L. A.D.S.S./Forms/C. 2118.

Instructions regarding War Diaries and Intelligence Summaries are contained in F. S. Regs., Part II. and the Staff Manual respectively. Title pages will be prepared in manuscript.

WAR DIARY
or
INTELLIGENCE SUMMARY.
(*Erase heading not required.*)

Army Form C. 2118.

Place	Date	Hour	Summary of Events and Information	Remarks and references to Appendices
1.2.15 D-------	1.		L. S. Horse (Canadians) Tr Inspection – 33 Limbered Wagons in bad condition. To be replaced. R C Dragoons (do) ADST & 10M present at Tr inspection – as for L.S.H. Straw x 1½ = 1 Hay.	
	2.		Canadian S Col arrived	
	3.		Canadian RHA Tr inspected with 10M. – Abbeville to see DDT southern –	
	4.		Canadian Bde HQ & Sig Tr Transport inspected with 10M.	
	5.		Canadian S Col began loading on 2 Echelon system & RP's ceased VB4 arrived from III Army	
	6.		Amtn Park rejoined from IIIrd Army	
	7.		Question of incorporation of M Amb Workshop being incorporated with DSCol Workshop reported unfavourably	
	8.		Past orders now communicated to new arrivals. Economy made in ASC supply. SSO returned from leave on 7th inst, MG sydus W.E. received,	
	9.		Permission to purchase potatoes & fodder beyond our area permitted – Went on leave & SSO as acting for me.	

2353 Wt. W2544/1454 700,000 5/15 D. D. & L. A.D.S.S./Forms/C. 2118.

Army Form C. 2118.

Instructions regarding War Diaries and Intelligence Summaries are contained in F. S. Regs., Part II. and the Staff Manual respectively. Title pages will be prepared in manuscript.

WAR DIARY
or
INTELLIGENCE SUMMARY.

(Erase heading not required.)

Place	Date	Hour	Summary of Events and Information	Remarks and references to Appendices
	10.2.16		Lt Colonel Norman Young proceeded on leave to England. Major E H Saunders acting OC ASC. All maps were checked	
	11.2.16		SSO went to railhead. Interviewed AASIT reference transport for Canadian Brigade	
	12.2.16		Visited Canadian Brigade with Captain Barnett and saw Staff Captain. handed in statements showing the Canadian Transport to be returned and amount of transport to be drawn from Abbeville. Captain Barnett (Adjt to OC ASC) to supervise the exchange. also prepared statements.	
	13.2.16		arranged rations to be sent to CONDE FOLIE for A battery RHA. rejoining Division on 14th. to be billeted at NIBAS. SSO visited railhead. 10 lbs hay ration resumed.	
	14.2.16		Canadian transport condemned and repairable carts being draught horses etc handed in at Abbeville fresh transport drawn to complete war establishment. A battery RHA arrived NIBAS. attached Mhow Brigade.	
	15.2.16		Refilling points for various units on main roads to obviate use of lorries and drivers on bad roads. The Adjutant visited Canadian Bde to assist 13th H.L.B. and Strathconas Horse OC RHA Canadian Bde transport re establishments & surplus carts etc. He also visited AASIT reference the above.	
	16.2.16		Further instructions received re use of side roads for lorries. Orders received regarding personnel for transport of Machine Gun Squadrons to be sent to Abbeville. The Adjutant saw Canadian transport re.... Canadian F. amb. arrived.	
	17.2.16		Digging party left for MONDICOURT and a 2nd digging party for DOULLENS. The Adjutant visited Canadian Bde arranged further periods for transport & instructed OC ASC Canadian Bde. Lt Col Young returned from leave.	

2353 Wt. W2544/1454 700,000 5/15 D. D. & L. A.D.S.S./Forms/C. 2118.

Instructions regarding War Diaries and Intelligence Summaries are contained in F. S. Regs., Part II. and the Staff Manual respectively. Title pages will be prepared in manuscript.

WAR DIARY
or
INTELLIGENCE SUMMARY.
(*Erase heading not required.*)

Army Form C. 2118.

Place	Date	Hour	Summary of Events and Information	Remarks and references to Appendices
18.2.16			Returned on 19th from leave – Adjt inspected visit to Canadian Tr, to clear up several points overlooked	
19.2.16			GOCDiv inspected L Bde Tr	
20.2.16			Instruction of Canadian O/C ASC in Tr – SSO visited Railhead	
21.2.16			M G Sqdns draw Tr at ABBEVILLE – Canadians returned horses to Regts & received their own by rail	
22.2.16			Instruction to BTO Canadian Bde in Tr – SSO to Railhead	
23.2.16			Thaw Scheme revised – Canadian ASC given instruction at their Bde HQ – Supply system when on the move	
24.2.16			Corps Comdrs orders re shoeing of animals.	
25.2.16			DS Coln to carry all spare sparking plugs except 1 per vehicle. Letter of appreciation DMT by Corps Comdr. Army Comdrs inspection. Ten tons straw to be bought from AILLY le HAUT CLOCHER	
26.2.16			Emergency Ration Statement to ADS&T.	
27.2.16			Thaw Scheme in operation tomorrow morning	
28.2.16			Indian Digging Party returned – Went to Railhead at 6 am & saw 46 [illegible] Park at Railhead to load.	
29.2.16			ADMS inspected reinforcements to DS Col, ASC & [illegible] road repair supervision.	

2353 Wt. W2544/1454 700,000 5/15 D. D. & L. A.D.S.S./Forms/C. 2118.

Instructions regarding War Diaries and Intelligence Summaries are contained in F. S. Regs., Part II. and the Staff Manual respectively. Title pages will be prepared in manuscript.

WAR DIARY
or
INTELLIGENCE SUMMARY.
(Erase heading not required.)

Army Form C. 2118.

Place	Date	Hour	Summary of Events and Information	Remarks and references to Appendices
1.4.16			Routine – held a conference of RQs to define the local resources & purchases. Broadly satisfactory & it is clear that the more we deal direct with vendors & the less the Mairies &c are introduced the better – the fewer "rings".	
2.4.16			LGS wagons taken over at Railhead by Adjt. 4 H Price to go to Egypt to Camel Corps.	
3.4.16			Conference at DDS&T's office at 2pm. General Jolait (Mission Française) in presence of all O/C ASC's (?) examined the Presidents of the Comites de Ravitaillement – The result was to put these two groups "in touch" – the whole proceedings seemed farcical (i) because in the SCOs we touch Mairies &c freely when it suits our buying work & (2) as in the past the obvious aim was to "organise" purchasing on both sides where we should organise & have vendors unorganised. There never is any friction with vendors – it is the "officials" who send up our rates. In China it was the same thing in the French & other forces – they got higher rates & yet vendors were not content – we gave lower rates & vendors were content. 2 more LGS wagons came in. SSM White acquitted by C.M.	
4.4.16			Capt Duke from SOBT to BTO Sialkote Bde. Capt Short SOBT. Summer scale of fuel begun with the option to maintain winter scale. Dried fruit & vegetables are weight for weight substitutes	
5.4.16			2 Surplus LGS wagons out of 11 sent (out of the 3 turnouts at Field Sqdn) returned to Third Army	
6.4.16			Glasses to obviate condensation of moisture on goggles with gas helmets. ASC supply 1 tin to 50 men weekly.	
7.4.16			GRO reduces jam from 4 to 3 ounces p.d. & increases milk tins from 16 to 12 men per tin. Pork etc. beans – Meat ration now 60% frozen at 1 lb & 25% Pres: at 3/4 lb now 4 days out of 7 + 15% P&B and Rsn M and 67 ? P.B. = 2 rations per tin. Once again the bad way of effecting sound alterations is resorted to. The scale is "amended" by formulae as above and no new print of Scale is issued.	
			SSO went on leave. L Bde go to Training area. 13th Rifle Bde demand special potatoes from Indian[illegible]	
8.4.16			Winter clothing surveyed by Bd Board. 6 Divisional receivers arrived. Instructions re NIV stores for Signal Troops & Studebaker self starters & [illegible] pressure pumps arrived	

WAR DIARY

or

INTELLIGENCE SUMMARY.

(Erase heading not required.)

Army Form C. 2118.

Instructions regarding War Diaries and Intelligence Summaries are contained in F. S. Regs., Part II. and the Staff Manual respectively. Title pages will be prepared in manuscript.

Place	Date	Hour	Summary of Events and Information	Remarks and references to Appendices
9.4.16			Visited DDS+T, who was out. Routine	
10.4.16			Potatoe sacks to be returned to Base. Cars reduced by SDOT's car – It seems to me a startling decision. Lime from Hesdin sold in a peculiar way which led to misinterpretation by M. Oliva – special memo placed on record & DDS+T (Inoculation Pos) informed	
11.4.16			An ingenious improvisation as dust protector for GS Wagons 200 wheels suggested. To be adopted by us. Warning that all potatoes sent via Railhead when buying ceases, buying can go on. Leather buckets for L G S wagons being abolished it is ordered that L G S fittings for them be removed	
12.4.16			Routine – Visited Railhead daily to do SSO's work	
13.4.16			Flame projector demonstration – looks very futile in action & even if much strengthened will be of little use against entrenched troops. Seems a useful thing for igniting an inflammable gas if latter could be pumped into an enemy's trench or store depot	
14.4.16			1. Bde return. S Bde go to training area. Visited DDS+T – out.	
15.4.16			Major Saunders returned from leave.	
16.4.16			Visited DD with SSO. Consulted him on lifters for Ambulances & HT + on spare parts. Also on Eclf of BSC now dismantled, also re coal deliveries + Butchery. All suggestions negatived because it is not	
17.4.16			sound to make any representations [crossed out] – Cycles [crossed out] understand are not to be necessary as this is defined already + M is being cut [crossed out]	

2353 Wt. W2544/1454 700,000 5/15 D. D. & L. A.D.S.S./Forms/C. 2118.

Army Form C. 2118.

WAR DIARY
or
INTELLIGENCE SUMMARY.
(Erase heading not required.)

Instructions regarding War Diaries and Intelligence Summaries are contained in F. S. Regs., Part II. and the Staff Manual respectively. Title pages will be prepared in manuscript.

Place	Date	Hour	Summary of Events and Information	Remarks and references to Appendices
18 4.16			Lt Beddoe DAP struck off (sick). T Lt R S C Wood replaces him. Base are asking why ASC [illegible] are attached to [illegible] Regts.	
19 4.16			Dl Training School stores ordered. Spare Limber hooks – DAC 1 MGS 3 Cav Regt 7.	
20.4.16			Orders for move of S Bde, M Bde & DHQ.	
21.4.16			Reps carts ordered out to units.	
22 4.16	Training Area St R.....		Moved to Training area. Dl Training is to go on to 7th prox.	
23 4.16			[illegible] Routine. Pork & Beans [illegible] additional issue of vegetables - fresh.	
24 4.16			Routine. Visited Railhead. Training continues - purely tactical	
25th –			Routine. Training	
26th –			No fuel agreements exist with us – the [illegible] enquiry indicates that they vary – [illegible] if we make any.	
27th –			Orders for summer scale of fuel [illegible] into force today.	
28th –			Rum now to be stopped.	
29th –			Routine only	
30th			Training going on. Purely tactical. We have today issued [illegible] Rations to practice units in pack. The training programme has throughout excluded all S & T work and it has been in [illegible] [illegible] owing to [illegible] overhaul [illegible] have 6 Bde areas – 3 permanent & 3 training + one [illegible] for overhaul [illegible]. There is an admin point here which was worth study but it is impossible to give any opinion of value now –	

2353 Wt. W2544/1454 700,000 5/15 D. D. & L. A.D.S.S./Forms/C. 2118.

Instructions regarding War Diaries and Intelligence Summaries are contained in F. S. Regs., Part II. and the Staff Manual respectively. Title pages will be prepared in manuscript.

WAR DIARY
or
INTELLIGENCE SUMMARY.
(Erase heading not required.)

Army Form C. 2118.

Place	Date	Hour	Summary of Events and Information	Remarks and references to Appendices
D..........	1/3		Thaw Scheme working with perfect smoothness; units exercising Sydis thro' the Refilling Point however seem to have a rooted conviction that they are quite justified in proceeding along no matter what they may disturb in spite of orders to the contrary. Scheme of despatch to obviate this difficulty.	
	4/3		Extra day suddenly ordered for Thaw Scheme which was duly continued except that hay lorries had to run, there being only 3 days hay stocked with units. Tip carts were found to be usable with HD horses. We have none so the carts could not be got from H T Depot. Decided not to draw them (for road repairing) as we may move before long. O/C + S.S.O visited Railhead. O/C visited Canadian Bde HQ + instructed ASC. S. Sgt Hollis decides to continue in service.	
	3/3.		Changed Lt Price & Lt Newnham as BTO's former from Mhow to Sialkot Bde. Ordered that no stores be bought outside any area except by permission thro D.H.Q. who are to obtain concurrence of French authorities.	
	4/3		Jodhpur Lancers attached to D Tr for S. T purposes. – Strength Br 27 Ind 717 Horses LD 650 – with 7 3-ton Daimlers	
	5/3,		+ 31 GDO's & each Set of DSC. This unit is truly a supply puzzle – Some Indian Officers draw Br Rations but Hindu or Mohdn meat (at Br scale)! They are composed of fluctuating groups (or retinues) & amorphous groups of officers, HQ, Rajahs, &c without War Estab or any defined nomenclature. "A Squadron" may mean anyone – Vocation of permutation & they throw off surprising detachments denominated for example "Rajah of Ratlam and retinue". To feed these will be a surprising feat if we do any work.	
	6/3		O/C ASC inspected Tr of S. Bde HQ + 6th Cav – Very fair – this Bde has broken out and daily with Lorry Reins – The system is R + D but they formed lorry reins & obtained them. Took this as a fair example of initiative as the system is understood by Silladar Cavalry. Repression of all such irregularities is demanded by a rigid system + is an obvious business necessity but they neither grasp this idea nor see the expediency of asking verbally for a BTO, much less of consulting O/C ASC or Q staff – Silladar Cavalry have the defect of their superlatively good training & qualities seen from the field Admin aspect & are apt to feel a little sore when thwarted. It seems to be a pity Kyth officers are not given some glimpse of Admin ideas & subjects beyond past practice esp in Tr matters.	

2353 Wt. W2544/1454 700,000 5/15 D. D. & L. A.D.S.S./Forms/C. 2118.

Instructions regarding War Diaries and Intelligence Summaries are contained in F. S. Regs., Part II. and the Staff Manual respectively. Title pages will be prepared in manuscript.

WAR DIARY

or

INTELLIGENCE SUMMARY.

(Erase heading not required.)

Army Form C. 2118.

Place	Date	Hour	Summary of Events and Information	Remarks and references to Appendices
	7.3.		O/C inspected Tr of 19 Lancers. Fair but saddlery not put on very well in some cases.	
			From 6 am today we are of Third Army but Fourth Army govern our Supply p.t. Third do the Tr [illegible].	
			Lt Jones leave extended to 20.3.16. Lt Burnett appointed to DSC [illegible] – Lt [illegible] struck off strength	
	8.3.		Lt Burnett arrived. 17th Lancers Tr inspected by O/CASC – very good. Tr of S Cav + [illegible] – good but they cling to the old	
			[illegible] cart with water tank – when not full of water it can carry kits. Three condemned [illegible] turned [illegible]	
			by O/CASC but unit has [illegible] the [illegible]. Next march I will see that that cart is [illegible].	
			O/CASC visited Cav: Bde for instruction	
			2 Troops draw own rations on H Tal Railhead – to economise petrol	
	9.3.		British Digging party – literally – [illegible] is quite unannounced from 36th Dn Corps Sy Sqdn + Mount [illegible] Depot attached	
			for rations ditto Lucknow Cav; Cleaning Stn. 2 LGOC Lorries attached to DSC to serve these LCCSth has own lorry	
			Visited DDS&T III Army – discussed various points re Railhead, Indian Butchery &c.	
			DSC is 47 Trained Drivers short – Q specially informed as a matter affecting efficiency of Dn	
			Scale of batmen + horses for BTO + BRO – one batman on a troop horse + one horse for officer	
	10/3		RTO + O/C DSC arranged direct without reporting to staff Reinforcements from Rd to units. Q + O/CASC arranged DAP	
	11.3		lorries – A small overlap not worth [illegible] for 10 M left over area	
			[illegible] Sqdn – 1 Tr returned from III Army Inf School. Capt [illegible] joined Dn on abolition of Corps HQ	
	12.3		Lectures on road repairs to ASC cancelled – a pity – Tr officers should certainly be instructed in hasty road repairs	
	13.3		O/C inspected Tr of Mhow Bde. Decidedly good – [illegible] (Cole BTO) much to be appreciated for this.	
	14.3		4 postal lorries re-allocated to the Dn. The area of a Cav Dn demands this in a civilised country – of which	
	15.3		spread out at least 1 per Bde (4 per Dn) in each Echelon will be necessary (8 in all) (+ spare 2)	

2353 Wt. W2544/1454 700,000 5/15 D. D. & L. A.D.S.S./Forms/C. 2118.

Instructions regarding War Diaries and Intelligence Summaries are contained in F. S. Regs., Part II. and the Staff Manual respectively. Title pages will be prepared in manuscript.

WAR DIARY
or
INTELLIGENCE SUMMARY.
(*Erase heading not required.*)

Army Form C. 2118.

Place	Date	Hour	Summary of Events and Information	Remarks and references to Appendices
	16.3.		350 [illegible] tailhead. I do not note this daily. The importance of observing Traffic Circuits & [illegible] is all [illegible]. It is one of those points perhaps scarcely emphasised enough in peace training. I fancy that all this subject [illegible] a useful study because there is probably a 'statistical' or 'principle' which are not yet clear even to those who compile the circuit maps & diagrams. This probably worth reducing to system.	
	17.3.		Smoke helmets being replaced. Steam (not house) coal to be issued to the Foden Lorry Disinfector – a [illegible] nuisance [illegible] have over 300 petrol motors & 1 steam nuisance. I [illegible] strongly and point [illegible] types. A designer could use exhaust heat for disinfecting or install a petrol [illegible] heater – there are splendid [illegible] in France – for heating to disinfect clothes – To plant a steam coal [illegible] is [illegible] stand at [illegible] and [illegible].	
	18.3.		Sgt [illegible] has withdrawn his application for a Course. [illegible] – We are [illegible]	
	19.3.		[illegible] 3 ton lorries to be issued to ASC in lieu of 6 [illegible] – stopped of 30 cwt lorries in favour of 3 ton lorries.	
	20.3.		[illegible] to [illegible] School [illegible] to reduce jam & add to tinned milk ration was sent for opinion. There should be some 'conversion' scheme calling all canned goods by net contents – we suffer from present nomenclature e.g. 1 Bolus, has 1 lb (nominal) 12 oz of tinned meat, 1 lb of tinned milk, 1 M & V Ration, – We should think speak & write of net weight in ounces – e.g. 12 oz tinned meat, milk &c [illegible] of the No. of oz per tin, which is variable but not liable to settle within an ounce for issue purposes.	
	21.3.		C/C inspected ~~[illegible]~~ Transport of [illegible] particularly good – Sgt [illegible] has done well. [illegible] – evidently good [illegible]	
	22.3.		C/C inspected [illegible] [illegible] MT [illegible] which [illegible] to their [illegible].	
	23.3.		Handed over ASC [illegible] Corps Sig Sqdn to [illegible] 26th unit.	
	24.3.		[illegible] The [illegible] Transport units.	

2353 Wt. W2544/1454 700,000 5/15 D. D. & L. A.D.S.S./Forms/C. 2118.

Instructions regarding War Diaries and Intelligence Summaries are contained in F. S. Regs., Part II. and the Staff Manual respectively. Title pages will be prepared in manuscript.

WAR DIARY

or

INTELLIGENCE SUMMARY.

(Erase heading not required.)

Army Form C. 2118.

Place	Date	Hour	Summary of Events and Information	Remarks and references to Appendices
[illegible] Marcq	25/3		[illegible] Cols [illegible] [illegible] [illegible]	
			[illegible]	
	26.3		[illegible]	
	27.3		[illegible] 13th Rifle Bde [illegible] 47 LD 9 H D [illegible]	
	28.3		[illegible]	
	29.3		[illegible] White [illegible]	
			[illegible]	
			[illegible]	
	30.3		[illegible]	
			[illegible]	
			[illegible]	
	31.3		[illegible]	
			[illegible]	

[illegible] Lt Col
O/C [illegible]

2353 Wt. W2544/1454 700,000 5/15 D. D. & L. A.D.S.S./Forms/C. 2118.

Instructions regarding War Diaries and Intelligence Summaries are contained in F. S. Regs., Part II. and the Staff Manual respectively. Title Pages will be prepared in manuscript.

WAR DIARY
or
INTELLIGENCE SUMMARY
(Erase heading not required.)

Army Form C. 2118

Place	Date	Hour	Summary of Events and Information	Remarks and references to Appendices
1.5.16			The AHT Coy is to have 33 Water tanks now being fitted but not mounted (200 galls per cart) Horse rugs withdrawn today. Purchases of fodder are to be made up to the value of shortages of hay @ £6 per ton.	
2.5.16			Training continues. Routine	
3.5.16			Ditto	
4.5.16			Tents to be stained before being pitched	
5.5.16			Routine	
6.5.16			DDS&T instructs that spares in one unit are considered available for any other unit under orders of the proper authority – D/C, Corps Comdr, A/C IC	
7.5.16			Returned to permanent area. GOC inspected DSC 1st Ech: & Workshops.	
8.5.16			Lorries of DSC may be used as busses. Amiens placed out of bounds. All road traffic to give way to Ry traffic on the roadside. Visited DDS&T regarding various points & to keep touch	
9.5.16			India decided that S.T Estabs not adversely reported on will be assumed to be fit for ordinary promotions. 2 3-ton lorries added to DAP for 18th and 1 for RHA	

1875 Wt. W593/826 1,000,000 4/15 J.B.C. & A. A.D.S.S./Forms/C. 2118.

Instructions regarding War Diaries and Intelligence Summaries are contained in F. S. Regs., Part II. and the Staff Manual respectively. Title Pages will be prepared in manuscript.

WAR DIARY
or
INTELLIGENCE SUMMARY
(Erase heading not required.)

Army Form C. 2118

Place	Date	Hour	Summary of Events and Information	Remarks and references to Appendices
9.5.16			S&T Reinforcements will now be demanded from DAG 2nd Sectn 3rd Echelon. Horseshoe nails – economy to be enforced & spares returned to Railhead.	
10.5.16			Moved to new area – inspected en route 1 Bde. D Tr & 1 Amb Tr. Visited Jodhpore Lancers, Inniskillen Dragoons, C I H in new billets. Mhow Bde B Echelon not being satisfactorily handled by B.T.O.	
11.5.16			Surplus stores (trench apron etc) brought on A H T carts. DSC detailed to send a car to School at AUXI. Fuel summer scale (1lb coke & ½lb charcoal) for men in trenches not in addition to but in lieu of coal.	
12.5.16			Visited DDS&T & B.T.O. Mhow will be changed. From today practically no M T used for supplies.	
13.5.16			Three Albion Lorries added to DAPk Estab for extra weight of 18 lb shells. Rum issues cease. Div: Mtd Bde Scheme received. Potatoes began to be rec from Base.	
14.5.16			O/C visited Railhead. Carts drawing there smoothly & well. Traffic control good as a start but can be improved. Am proceeding on leave tomorrow. Major Saunders acts as O/C DSC	

1875 Wt. W593/826 1,000,000 4/15 J.B.C. & A. A.D.S.S./Forms/C. 2118.

Instructions regarding War Diaries and Intelligence Summaries are contained in F. S. Regs., Part II. and the Staff Manual respectively. Title pages will be prepared in manuscript.

WAR DIARY
or
INTELLIGENCE SUMMARY.

(*Erase heading not required.*)

Army Form C. 2118.

Place	Date	Hour	Summary of Events and Information	Remarks and references to Appendices
Field	[illegible]		[illegible]	
	16.5.16		[illegible]	
	17.5.16		[illegible]	
	18.5.16		[illegible]	
	19.5.16		[illegible]	
	20.5.16		[illegible]	
	21.5.16		[illegible]	
	22.5.16		[illegible]	
	23.5.16		[illegible]	
	24.5.16		[illegible]	
	25.5.16		[illegible]	
	26.5.16		[illegible]	
	27.5.16		[illegible]	

2353 Wt. W2544/1454 700,000 5/15 D. D. & L. A.D.S.S./Forms/C. 2118.

Instructions regarding War Diaries and Intelligence Summaries are contained in F. S. Regs., Part II. and the Staff Manual respectively. Title Pages will be prepared in manuscript.

WAR DIARY
or
INTELLIGENCE SUMMARY
(Erase heading not required.)

Army Form C. 2118

Place	Date	Hour	Summary of Events and Information	Remarks and references to Appendices
28.5.16			Returned from leave. [illegible] School [illegible] yesterday. D.D.S.&T. inspected [illegible] (found in perfectly satisfactory & decidedly creditable condition) & A. H.T. Coy. – All horses [illegible] returned from work or were resting on relief from units. The lines carts & harness good. The horses seen were not showy & I gathered that [illegible] understood what they represented. Personally I think the Vety Branch are not overrating freely enough & [illegible] this to O/C A.H.T. Coy & to their Vety attendants. The A.H.T. Coy are very hard worked but are giving them 15 lbs oats.	
29.5.16			School are to have a Lorry p.t. for daily duty. Routine. ~~[illegible]~~	
30.5.16			Went to St Pol with O/C H.T. & Supply Park re Loading Table. Believe that this will result in a better arrangement. B.T.O. [illegible] Bde's case discussed. There is here a slight point of some use to note on broadly. It might be well to prevent O/C's [illegible] men in [illegible] positions more freely – i.e. without reflecting fatally on their right [illegible] relief. The point is [illegible] & needs a very careful consideration & a regulation.	
31.5.16			Went to Railhead with S.S.O. – S.S.O. is arranging with R.S.O. to receive all parties of [illegible] letter can [illegible] before [illegible] acting for him when sudden reinforcements arrive. Letter [illegible] [illegible] them for S.S.O.'s disposal – the credit comes on 3.3.16. It is [illegible] to assume that R can warn S.S.O. of all arrivals but as a system the assumption can be met & [illegible] dealt with if R.S.O. cooperates. A. M. Young Lt Col CRASC [illegible]	

1875 Wt. W593/826 1,000,000 4/15 J.B.C. & A. A.D.S.S./Forms/C. 2118.

Instructions regarding War Diaries and Intelligence Summaries are contained in F. S. Regs., Part II. and the Staff Manual respectively. Title Pages will be prepared in manuscript.

WAR DIARY
or
INTELLIGENCE SUMMARY
(Erase heading not required.)

Army Form C. 2118

Place	Date	Hour	Summary of Events and Information	Remarks and references to Appendices
1.6.16			All mounted men except vehicle drivers to have wallets. All unser: clothing to be returned to Ord: not destroyed.	
2.6.16			Lieut Haig arrived – Did not report his arrival or join BSOs mess. is far over 50 yrs of age & unable to walk from gout. Appointed Brigade Transport Officer – Was applied for for this purpose by GOC Mhow Bde.	
3.6.16			Res: Park H.T ordered to comply with order forbidding name & number of formations on signboards. ADMS asked to issue orders to a C.F.'s amb to act as retailer of Medical comforts	
4.6.16			Salvage Squadron formed. Res Park H T to examine Br Eur: Ration Grocery tins to ascertain no Oxo cubes remain [these cubes melt & cake the tea sugar &c – now obsolete]. Fittings arrived for the tanks for A H T Coy [the carts are to be fitted with 200 gal water tanks of corrugated iron – memo this function of Tr. should be weighed when designing a G.S. vehicle – it seems likely to be increasingly recognised as a F.S. necessity]	
5.6.16			Lucknow Bde Tr inspected – K.D.G. 29th Cav &c all good – 36th J H not so good but quite as serviceable & quite tolerably turned out. Regtl T.O. as usual changed. It is doubtful whether Regts will ever realise [& tho' I try to press it home to them it is becoming clear to me that the system is wrong in trying to make them realise] that Transport is important enough to cause them to demand fixity of tenure of RTO for a few months – junior officers all want to be with their squadrons & it is a delusion to organise on these lines. The Tr service should provide each Regt on Mobn [or in peace arrange to train men of the Regt] with a Sergt – who could then do the work no matter how the R.T.O. neglected the Tr. The BTOs are the one personal standby & he has to be very tactful to influence Regtl Tr. Officers. The excellent material & an occasional extra ordinary Regtl TO – a Yeomanry officer perhaps helps out – & inspections help. But Ind Cavy Regts should not be allowed Tr. on charge without a Tr. NCO of some standing to do the supervisory work. I am very thankful we have Indian RHA Drivers in some numbers for they have proved useful indeed & shown the way in every unit.	

Instructions regarding War Diaries and Intelligence Summaries are contained in F. S. Regs., Part II. and the Staff Manual respectively. Title Pages will be prepared in manuscript.

WAR DIARY
or
INTELLIGENCE SUMMARY
(Erase heading not required.)

Army Form C. 2118

Place	Date	Hour	Summary of Events and Information	Remarks and references to Appendices
5.6.16 cont			Inspected office of SODT – All satisfactory. Capt Short SODT tells me Condr Gale is improved in value & manner but I gather elsewhere that it would be well to move him. He is a valuable man in his position but prides himself on being outspoken & calling a spade a spade but it involves roughness approximating to objections to orders & mistaken obstinateness & much unnecessary friction – 3 cases last month & another instance came to my knowledge today. Twice warned & ~~we~~ he must go. 200 Grocery tins sent to dump to be reissued. Lieut Haig has assumed duties of BTO Mhow Bde.	
6.6.16			All potatoes & onions now to come from Base – purchases cease. The Park arrived with Atta in lieu of biscuits – bags and tins – change to biscuits sanctioned – to be done from Railhead. Mules are now to be classified as 'large' or 'small' on B 213. All our mules are really large – i.e. over 15 hands – as regards work but by measure a few with low withers may just fall short – & may be cut down to 6 lbs oats – We have authority to ~~feed~~ draw 12 per animal tho' out the Dn & I hope this is not to be altered. It is a mistake to classify animals one way for work & another way for food – the terms are far more nearly connected than a single linear measurement is with either the bulk or power or maintenance 'units of nutrition' – or work capabilities or work performance. An animal classified for x work should get x class rations & not Z class rations.	
7.6.16			Visited HT Res Park – CM's going on – a rough gang included in this unit. Arranged Jodhpore Durbar billets. Inspected Sialkote Bde Tr. All satisfactory – 6th Cav'y Tr dirty carts, new Regtl TO. 17th Lancers very good & 19th the same. Conference re area between front line & B Ech for Cav'y on normal operations – Best conference I have attended yet – a clear discussion & decision on every point & clear notes & orders arranged in a brief time by reasonable compromises. Areas (a) fighting front (b) Collecting area (c) B Echelon (d) Railhead – certain units & details defined and a system for notifying & handling & rationing stragglers, prisoners, &c fixed up.	
~~8.6.16~~				

1875 Wt. W593/826 1,000,000 4/15 J.B.C. & A. A.D.S.S./Forms/C. 2118.

Instructions regarding War Diaries and Intelligence Summaries are contained in F. S. Regs., Part II. and the Staff Manual respectively. Title pages will be prepared in manuscript.

WAR DIARY
or
INTELLIGENCE SUMMARY
(Erase heading not required.)

Army Form C. 2118.

Hour, Date, Place	Summary of Events and Information	Remarks and references to Appendices
8.6.16	Routine – no questions of interest cropped up	
9.6.16	Visited DDS&T. Compiled suggested Loading Table for H T Res S Park. Discussed Lt Haigs appt and mentioned that I had seen Capt Cowdell at Boulogne doing nothing – no work of any sort for over a month.	
10.6.16	A H-T Coy is to have 7 additional GS Wagons & more limbers perhaps.	
11.6.16	Lime juice 1/320 gals to be issued in lieu of green vegetables & onions if not available, on Med: advice. The ration, substitutes & extras scale requires to be issued corrected to date. Rubber sponge goggles provided for lorry & car drivers (anti lachrymatory gas)	
12.6.16	1 officer & 50 men Br. detached for Regt to join 51st Div. DDS&T asked to check flow of vegetables by rail to avoid prolonged storage at dump. Inspected 3 C F A's Tr – extremely good & a show which Irish Regts could see.	
13.6.16	Conference ordered of Brigadiers, O/C ASC & O/C Fd Sqdn re pack Tr – 26 officers attended & some tentative suggestions discussed – no decisions – I was asked no questions – took opportunity to decoy 2 Regtl officers aside to show them how they load mules – 1 had a camp kettle poised on top so that its edge cut vertically into the horses backbone, longitudinally between the pads & the other had two pick heads sticking into the animals flanks – It is astonishing how fluent some men are in talking over subjects they obviously have never studied – I listened today to an officer describing a load to the Bde GOC ~~[illegible]~~ – from actual experience on field service noticed on the spot. I am fully convinced that modern military study & modern equipments [illegible] them to learn about except as an amateur. To expect	

Instructions regarding War Diaries and Intelligence Summaries are contained in F. S. Regs., Part II. and the Staff Manual respectively. Title pages will be prepared in manuscript.

WAR DIARY
or
INTELLIGENCE SUMMARY

(Erase heading not required.)

Army Form C. 2118.

Hour, Date, Place	Summary of Events and Information	Remarks and references to Appendices
	a Regtl officer not to bluff that he is an expert all round is vain & leads to an obscuring of the facts of such a matter as pack Tr. I mentioned to A.A. & Q.M.G. as a matter of form that it would be well to use the trained S.&T. men to help Regtl pack transport questions thro' – but as he says Silladar Regts have grass mules in India & all their officers know all about pack Transport – It is technical transport & not A.S.C. & not in my purview to inspect it – Will have a try to advise later. This is noted in some detail as it may come in useful when reorganisation questions arise & attempt is made to imagine F.S. conditions & circumstances – Incidentally it may serve to explain why after the first few days of a march the heavy tally of sorebacks &c tends to fall to normal. The fact really is that the Regimental training & atmosphere leads naturally to tactics & not to admin questions such as Tr & it is only after marches have forced attention to them that the inexpert supervisor & men take the – really very simple – precautions which the 'expert' would advise – if listened to. All my experience here points to the hollowness of an organisation which does not include an S&T repr. within each unit. To 'interfere' with a unit from outside is very difficult, to cause a representative to be a most useful adviser & stand by to the O/C is quite easy. It is fallacious to suppose that the Regimental officer unless his prospects depend on admin work [of QM of a Bn unit] will average out as a tolerable Tr officer. The Indian units that I see have persistently changed Tr officers who	

Instructions regarding War Diaries and Intelligence Summaries are contained in F. S. Regs., Part II. and the Staff Manual respectively. Title pages will be prepared in manuscript.

WAR DIARY
or
INTELLIGENCE SUMMARY
(Erase heading not required.)

Army Form C. 2118.

Hour, Date, Place	Summary of Events and Information	Remarks and references to Appendices
	always "don't want to be T.O." & try hard to get out of it. It is a fact that in a few weeks a Temp[y] officer makes a better B.T.O. than an officer of 10 years service in a Silladar reg[t] makes of R.T.O.s job – viewed from the Tr aspect.	
14.6.16.	Today loading at 6 am & also clocks put on 1 hr to Summer time at 11 pm. Visited Railhead with S.S.O. who goes daily.	
15.6.16	1 section of H. Park joined 37th D[n] empty – loads dumped. (20 wagons) 52 lorries used outside D[n] / Sunbeam Car sent to Div of Cavalry.	
16.6.16	Capt Watson A.S.C. who goes round 'saving' – He came to this D[n] without letting us know & has been questioning various junior officers & O.R. & I hear he has saved £170,000 worth of glycerine from 'waste cookhouse products' – He asked some questions of the Innisk: Dragoons which produced replies from which any S[t] service officer could have saved him. He was told that "biscuits were not short drawn because bread might be cut & they wanted all the bread as per scale" – I went round to the Reg[t] on hearing this & found it was a fact that this reply had been given. Examination of indents showed that this Reg[t] had never had their bread cut & were aware it never would be cut by this D[n] S[y] service but in 1914 & early '15 in another D[n] it had been done & this is what the Q.M. "had in mind". I said all right but [illegible]	

Army Form C. 2118.

Instructions regarding War Diaries and Intelligence Summaries are contained in F. S. Regs., Part II. and the Staff Manual respectively. Title pages will be prepared in manuscript.

WAR DIARY
or
INTELLIGENCE SUMMARY.
(Erase heading not required.)

Place	Date	Hour	Summary of Events and Information	Remarks and references to Appendices
			think you should short draw some biscuits now you are with us" – The instantaneous reply was "The men make puddings of them & we want every ounce" They had no stock – never weighed an ounce & would not short draw their "pudding" – Now the Director of [illegible] is sure to feel he is on to quite a big question – This (as he will not guess) has an exact parallel in Atta + Biscuits + in "frozen meat & bully beef" – and we have legislated & enforced the proper safeguards against cutting bread, atta, & frozen meat when biscuits, & bully are short indented for – We did this a very long time ago. This illustrates the result of sending round inexperienced young men to dig into the results of experienced mens work behind their backs. Besides the nonsense they gather along with sound facts it makes (as in this case) BSO's &c feel 'spied upon' by men who have to 'justify their existence' & it makes everyone feel that ones reputation is at the mercy of any young ass allowed to run at large & browse on thistles & personally I feel inclined to ask for another such to be sent to find out when I am consulted – Anyone of the S+T service could have put this in a clear light but the young man has disappeared & doubtless is composing a report on the discovery in the Dn that we do not know our job – The 6th Dn no more hesitate to short draw than any other [illegible] & we have as a Dn short drawn hundreds of tons of biscuits & bully	
17.6.16			300 men per I C R as digging party – Visited their new Dn + saw Offg O/C Train re[illegible] for vegetables, refilling point billets &c – much struck by difference of ASC practice & our own – in the points observed we have further proof of the difference in fundamental principles we work on	

2353 Wt. W2544/1454 700,000 5/15 D. D. & L. A.D.S.S./Forms/C. 2118.

Instructions regarding War Diaries and Intelligence Summaries are contained in F. S. Regs., Part II. and the Staff Manual respectively. Title pages will be prepared in manuscript.

WAR DIARY
or
INTELLIGENCE SUMMARY.
(Erase heading not required.)

Army Form C. 2118.

Place	Date	Hour	Summary of Events and Information	Remarks and references to Appendices
18.6.16.			S.S.O. arranged to suit digging parties lorries & supplies. Routine	
19.6.16			Lt Tredcroft MT ASC given commission as Lt in Sp Res of O. AO/ No car to go outside Dn area without pass from DHQ. T. Lorries to the "Dl Troops". It took 7 lorries to disperse the Dl school.	
20.6.16			AHT Coy carts withdrawn from units. Lt Risley reports arrival Capt Payne to go to 73 Corps Tr & S. Coln. Vegetable consignments stopped via DDS&T – but still they arrive. We have 3 weeks stock.	
21.6.16			Visited AHT Coy who are fixing up tanks – These have given some anxiety – pity they did not think of sail canvas bags & cart lining. Vety Insp. DHQ Tr & ASC horses. Vety Officer says they are best in the Dn – they are all right. GOC Lucknow Bde under a letter by O/C 29th & 36th suggests tinned meat for Indians. AA & QMG refers to me & wants this squashed once more. The GOC has never been in India & has some regtl officers who constantly tackle this question – a very different one – Atta was sanctioned & abandoned as an emergency ration for cooking reasons. So biscuits were settled on to go with the ½ lb gur. We have tried bully mutton – but it will not do first the wrappers have as a trade mark a cow or bullocks head. Secondly the wrappers wash off & the tins are similar to beef tins – this affects Hindus whilst the Mohms simply wont touch it as it has not been hallalled – They do in some Regts vow they want it but when made available they leave it about & we have to rush out gur in lieu. I believe the solution of this question may be the issue of a Ration tin which each Regt can fill with SHAKARPARA either issued as cooked by L of C or by the Regts – Atta gur & ghi being the ingredients. At this place & date adherence to Biscuits 1 lb & gur ½ lb is the only plan.	

Instructions regarding War Diaries and Intelligence Summaries are contained in F. S. Regs., Part II. and the Staff Manual respectively. Title pages will be prepared in manuscript.

WAR DIARY
or
INTELLIGENCE SUMMARY.
(Erase heading not required.)

Army Form C. 2118.

Place	Date	Hour	Summary of Events and Information	Remarks and references to Appendices
22.6.16			21 G.S. Wagons with Bde H.Q. tools added to Dn. All arrived as usual without any accessories, 7 Water tanks & S.W. stores from Abbeville	
			Conference at D.H.Q. Reported total of 40 tanks all ready. These are sure to leak badly on rough roads with springless vehicles	
23.6.16			Br. Regts digging parties return. 1 Wheeler 2 farriers & 6 spare drivers added to W.E. of A.H.T. Coy at length after many representations.	
24.6.16			We are cutting Batteries etc to 12 lbs oats & I.C. Regts to 11 to save 5 lbs per horse in Dn as extra emergency Ration in nosebags.	
25.6.16			2 Days F.R. biscuits carried about with a view to emergency measures to yield the provision of [illegible] now distributed to men for carriage on person, pack & A Ech Tr. This is bring raised a very important point for it seems likely to be a permanent organization feature for Cav: as an arm — It is clear in war but not in peace and I particularly recommend this point for study in connection with the use, mobility & maintenance of Cav: in action. I have pressed it here for a very long time & it is admitted now as an 'emergent Transport' basis — the animals equipment distribution incidents to improvised of course but it demands thought & provision in reorganising Cav: later on. It has never been a 'fad' but emerged in the course of working out plans in the field, during constant movements & with action impending & has tricked up to the Staff as a practical strengthening of Cavalry.	
26.6.16			L of C ask if biscuits will do in lieu of [illegible] for voyage rations — yes (after inquiry) except for C.F.A. Rations who will take atta in lieu —	
			Dumped all vegetables except a few days issues, in the Dn Dump.	

Instructions regarding War Diaries and Intelligence Summaries are contained in F. S. Regs., Part II. and the Staff Manual respectively. Title pages will be prepared in manuscript.

WAR DIARY
or
INTELLIGENCE SUMMARY
(Erase heading not required.)

Army Form C. 2118.

Hour, Date, Place	Summary of Events and Information	Remarks and references to Appendices
27.6.16	All digging parties return – Car lent to School returned to DSC –	
28.6.16	All but Batteries & RHA DAC returned. These rejoin on 30th. Sanction obtained to issue 1oz (3 days) extra of Tea to Ind. Tr to add to their 3 days Iron Ration. These orders received by Dn Rv, not [illegible] – It has been discussed & settled that OCDSC should be at DHQ & not with B Ech. For this reason in anticipation I appointed Capt Duke a BTO – he now commands "B" – this omission in orders is an illustration ~~[illegible]~~ – in this case after examining traffic orders & moving lines [illegible] Rv. to suit – ~~[illegible]~~. In the Home Orgn every formation has an ASC Q officer who does Q work the other Q branch man does the A work – so far as I know?	
29.6.16	The question of transfer of establishment [illegible] for Admin purposes is a very simple process by the current system but so far we have never once had a sudden transfer to this Dn which has gone properly – This process demands a collected group of instructions in detail – the instructions are scattered & are never complied with – we are keen on this process as it has been our fate to send many detachments to other fmns & one has been able to observe this small loose screw & set it right at our end. The coordination & channels of comn for 'transfers' & not the other details are the points which are lost sight of – G do not tell Q & Q forgets to tell the other formation in time or lorry transfers are not ordered through correct channels	
30th 6.16	Moved to D - - - - - - - area. Bdes independently. Saw Tr on way. One cart abused by S MG Sqdn – took details, dumped half the load by wayside & reported case – a flagrant one. We move very light & easy this time & the	

1247 W 3299 200,000 (E) 8/14 J.B.C. & A. Forms/C. 2118/11.

Instructions regarding War Diaries and Intelligence Summaries are contained in F. S. Regs., Part II. and the Staff Manual respectively. Title pages will be prepared in manuscript.

WAR DIARY
or
INTELLIGENCE SUMMARY
(Erase heading not required.)

Army Form C. 2118.

Hour, Date, Place	Summary of Events and Information	Remarks and references to Appendices
	change is pleasant. DM's created an amusing & typical case 17th Lancers asked for 80 men's and horses at DM's place – they however sent 30 men 44 horses & mules! Result was the Regtl HQ complained (verbally) of being 50 rations short – they are very good indeed – our best regiment in accuracy of work & unfailing smartness in grasping what to do to help the A.S.C. & this is an instance of how easily an 'acting' hand can create bother – we had to run a lorry to Railhead & must adjust tomorrow & had this sort of thing cropped up when far from Railhead 50 men's rations would have been short in the field. I am all for an Admin service estab attached to each Regt instead of a Regtl estab:– but recognize that this has drawbacks.	
	This month I have ventured to record impressions on a few points rather freely as we are now far more 'regular' than heretofore & have evolved an interior routine of some Admin interest – I record it as I see it & think of it from time to time in the light of experience such as I have. It is not my intention to reflect on anyone's opinions or actions – merely to assist consideration in after days perhaps	
	H. M. Young MC Lt-Col S & TC OC RASC ...	

1247 W 3299 200,000 (E) 8/14 J.B.C. & A. Forms/C. 2118/11.

Army Form C. 2118.

Instructions regarding War Diaries and Intelligence Summaries are contained in F. S. Regs., Part II. and the Staff Manual respectively. Title pages will be prepared in manuscript.

WAR DIARY
or
INTELLIGENCE SUMMARY
(Erase heading not required.)

In accordance with G 237 d/3.R.16 from DHQ

Hour, Date, Place	Summary of Events and Information	Remarks and references to Appendices
1.7.16 DOULLENS.	⅓ oz tea p. man p. diem to be added to the 3 days Emergency Rations for Indians which are carried (1) on the man under rule (2) on the man as a special local rule (3) on cooks carts & packs as a special local rule. Sugar was not suggested the gur at ½ lb per man being available. A fatigue party for the Dn Dump at railhead had to be detailed. This must be virtually a permanent party & under this system it might better be of non combatant classes – about 15 physically efficient untrained labourers per Dn seems the useful minimum.	
2.7.16	18th Cie 5me GENIE FRANCAISE applied for & were given rations in the Dn. Move of whole Dn from DOULLENS area to AUXI area on orders to move at once. Nothing abnormal beyond a noteworthy facility of movement due to the institution of a dump for the clearance of various equipments & used for training, billet, winter &c purposes. Under 2½ hours notice – B sub wagons not available for local supplies at any distance from a units billet. Amb: motors to be covered with screens of expanded metal as superstructure over the canvas. Latter expected to be 'rubbed' into holes.	
3.7.16 AUXI LE CHATEAU	Dis-mounted men move from REBREUVE near FREVENT R'h'd to AUXI It is worth while considering the idea of giving 1 GSW per 100 men (DM's) in connection with the fact that they are 'spare' men whilst we have not one single 'spare' GSW in the Divn under W. Estab. DM's GSW would be in use for DM's, for drawing Rations [in lieu of lorries] & would during operations be a useful source for rapid renewal of breakdowns in the field pending replacement from L of C. Additional eq'mt is however not desirable generally – point noted as of interest.	

1247 W 3299 200,000 (E) 8/14 J.B.C. & A. Forms/C. 2118/11.

Army Form C. 2118.

Instructions regarding War Diaries and Intelligence Summaries are contained in F. S. Regs., Part II. and the Staff Manual respectively. Title pages will be prepared in manuscript.

WAR DIARY
or
INTELLIGENCE SUMMARY
(Erase heading not required.)

Hour, Date, Place	Summary of Events and Information	Remarks and references to Appendices
4.7.16 – AUXI	Field Cashier moved to Railhead as convenient central point whence he can be reached – any unit or Bde – daily. Note this is due to Cav^y D.S.C. org^n + is not applicable to an Inf. D^n Returned surplus publications to Stationery Dept. Might be legislated for as publications must always tend to accumulate in the field + be destroyed, lost or carried about unnecessarily unless from the start the point is clearly understood + correct action defined	
5.7.16. AUXI	Sgt HORNBY S.T.C. joined Mhow Bde S.O.; Estab from ROUEN. D M's rejoined their units. It has been decided that O/C ASC should accompany D.H.Q. to control S.T services + arrange suitable Comdr for B. Echelon. Consequential provision for horses and equipment made to provide an "officers group". This point is worth noting as it arises from relative ease of control from D H Q compared with B Echelon position + it avoids sudden variation of method on leaving billets for operations – O/C + SSO thus retain their functions + methods + arrangement of work throughout unchanged + the channel of orders AQMG – O/C ASC – SSO – BSOs + Rhd is not modified by O/C dropping out + thus in fact [tho not in theory] losing real responsibility + control directly operations begin. An S.T O – appointed B.T.O. so as to command B Ech + stand ready if nec: to replace a BSO casualty. Adjt remains with B Echelon. Cube iron tanks instead of corrugated sheet iron cylindrical tanks [both 200 gls] arrived for Aux. H.T. Coy – to be fitted as can be devised on the spot by O/C Field Sqdn RE + O/C ASC.	
6.7.16. AUXI	Marseilles enquiring thro' L of C whether Indian sea rations [non cooking] may conform to Emergency rations in substituting biscuits for gram – Enquiries BSO's informed all units concur except 100 Kahars – who want atta or	

1247 W 3299 200,000 (E) 8/14 J.B.C. & A. Forms/C. 2118/11.

Instructions regarding War Diaries and Intelligence Summaries are contained in F. S. Regs., Part II. and the Staff Manual respectively. Title pages will be prepared in manuscript.

WAR DIARY
or
INTELLIGENCE SUMMARY
(Erase heading not required.)

Army Form C. 2118.

Hour, Date, Place	Summary of Events and Information	Remarks and references to Appendices
	Chenna chabena – These men are the source of the original idea of instituting a variety of SHAKARPARA as the emergency rations for all Indians. It appears to follow that this ration would be suitable for board ship also as the non-cooking + stormy weather issue – Various small similar experiences are convincing me that this substance probably would solve the doubts + recurrent difficulties connected with an Iron ration for Indian Troops.	
7.7.16. AUXI	Railhead ordered for tomorrow at PETIT HOUVIN.– Anti gas sprayers 4 to be carried. 1 each Ech of DSC + 2 on 2 Tool carts moving with DHQ – Thus 2 always with DHQ – 1 available at 1st Ration issue + 1 with DHQ A Ech: 24 hours later – In view of use of gas in war + of cases where sudden additional equipments may be [as always] required to be carried an advantage + no waste would be the result of adhering to the principle of providing in wagon loading tables an acknowledged margin of spare power – equipments are at times necessarily ordered – the corresponding carrying power has to be 'found' by existing transport. It works out at either overloading or unacknowledged transport or dispensing with some other equipment – the result is want of uniformity + its train of difficulties – often small – always recurrent.	
8.7.16. AUXI	Daily wire stating balance of vegetables in hand instituted. – Railhead PETIT HOUVIN Routine	
9.7.16 —	Lt POLE [to 15th B Train] relieved by Lt BRITTS [reinforcement] in 1st ICD H.T Res: Park	
10.7.16 —	Office records sent to "Records" for safe custody – see note dated 4.7.16 Bread truck broken down on RY at CONTEVILLE cleared by our lorries – example of the way lorry power retrieves accidents + keeps troops regularly at full normal ration scale.	
11.7.16 —	2 BOs + 50 Ind O.R. returned on train proceeding to Review at Paris B	

1247 W 3299 200,000 (E) 8/14 J.B.C. & A. Forms/C. 2118/11.

Instructions regarding War Diaries and Intelligence Summaries are contained in F. S. Regs., Part II. and the Staff Manual respectively. Title pages will be prepared in manuscript.

WAR DIARY
or
INTELLIGENCE SUMMARY
(Erase heading not required.)

Army Form C. 2118.

Hour, Date, Place	Summary of Events and Information	Remarks and references to Appendices
12.7.16 AUXI.	Small fishhook found in an oat sack – not the pattern indicated in warning – obviously a chance case – details blurred by inexact track of how & where & in what position it was discovered. We test oats occasionally with toy magnets which I think would extract small iron or steel objects – no result so far. In case of foreign supplies of grain magnets (pocket size but rather well magnetised – say 4 oz horse shoe shape with keeper) would be worth providing at bases. The test in the field seems out of place – examination by eye for objects intended to kill horses is a point for stable management – Points of equipment & precautions – suggested.	
13.7.16 AUXI	Camouflaging Transport wagons [B Echn] in lieu of authorised G.S. colour decided on. Muddy brown picked out with [20% of area] green marks of various shapes alternate spokes & felloe spaces green & brown adopted for the Dn. Eases demand for the one GS paint, facilitates using local resources – distinguishes the DL carts	
14.7.16 } 15.7.16 } AUXI	Routine	
16.7.16. —	S&TC – Arrivals S/t HORNBY from ROUEN, S/c Crowley, S/S Thompson, S/Duggan from Base Marseilles. Departures S/c Gale, S/KEEFE to Marseilles.	
17.7.16	2 BOs & 50 Ind OR returned from Review at Paris. U By + 1 Gun Secn DAC	
18.7.16	joined 5th Dn IV Army with 15 Indians. The inclusion of Indians in small numbers in Br units does not quâ orgn stand the test of f.s. in Europe under the current system. Units have got rid of this difficulty except RHA Batteries who remain presenting a difficulty in interchangeability & supply which seems certainly out of all proportion to the difference by which these 15 Indians excel 15 British with similar duties perhaps. The point brings out an orgn principle perhaps,	

1247 W 3299 200,000 (E) 8/14 J.B.C. & A. Forms/C. 2118/11.

Army Form C. 2118.

Instructions regarding War Diaries and Intelligence Summaries are contained in F. S. Regs., Part II. and the Staff Manual respectively. Title pages will be prepared in manuscript.

WAR DIARY
or
INTELLIGENCE SUMMARY
(Erase heading not required.)

Hour, Date, Place	Summary of Events and Information	Remarks and references to Appendices
19.7.16	Move to MINGOVAL + VILLERSCHATEL. No important points.	
20.7.16. Villers CHATEL	BTOs called on for special reports on wheels after yesterdays long march — reports satisfactory — dry weather producing no abnormal effect — attributable to good wheels & strawing round axle — some units use old gunny loosely twisted into ropes laced thro spokes round hub — RAILHEAD — TINCQUES.	
21.7.16 – 24.7.16 — " —	Routine	
25.7.16.	Rules re HAY & its weights of Admin: interest. Today to quote. Weighments forbidden waybills [based on shipping notes] to be accepted as giving average weights of bales. Units base representations on actual weighments proving local shortage — thus the onus of dividing equitably rests on judging bales at Railhead — almost impossible to prevent all cases of under & over supply — Apart from Pack transport questions there is great advantage here in expending substantial sums on securing as far as possible uniformity of weight — & failing this size of bale is less important than uniformity of density — varied sizes can be judged only if of uniform density.	
2	Possibly disinfector machines may be considered in future as a Field Amb: vehicle. As a vehicle without animals allotted to it, it is an abnormal item to watch. The existence of a Sanitary Section apart from Amb: & a disinfector ditto present petty complication in S & T detail work. The Salvage Sqdn, ditto.	
26.7.16	Disinfector fuel is 'steam' coal — only unit requiring this owing to pattern of furnace.	
27.7.16	Sgt Springfield interviewed by GOC Dn with a view to Commission.	
28–30/7/16	Routine	
31.7.16	Reserve Park gas training & test.	

[signature] Lt Col
O/C ASC [illegible] Dn.

Army Form C. 2118.

Instructions regarding War Diaries and Intelligence Summaries are contained in F. S. Regs., Part II. and the Staff Manual respectively. Title pages will be prepared in manuscript.

WAR DIARY
or
INTELLIGENCE SUMMARY.

(Erase heading not required.)

Place	Date	Hour	Summary of Events and Information	Remarks and references to Appendices
1.8.16			No more motor ambulances to be metalled over. Gas attacks – importance emphasized in a circular. A case of special permission to run contrary to traffic arrow [to save petrol] has been given. 2nd Lancers feel scarcity of water & 4 A H T Coy W. carts attached to them. SSO went on leave. O/C acting. SD Ind: per regt rationed 5 days by rail to the Base. 23 lbs meat found bad in Regt – hot weather & flies. We had to weigh this probability when deciding not to incur drawbacks of moving the butchery from Adv Base Rouen. Frozen meat all right thro' any weather.	
2.8.16			Important circular re petrol economy. Reexamined this question. Carts draw from Railhead when possible & we are doing a good deal to ensure economy. DSC & DAP are careful – impressed O/C's on this point verbally & sent on circular. Small economies depend on local & unit care now. The bigger measures taken. Wired Base that Indians rationed up to & for 5th inst by Rail yesterday.	
3.8.16.			Visited Railhead. 7 ~~[illegible]~~ tanks & spares arrived for AHT Coy. Leather diaphragms to be made up locally. 4 cwt coal extra weekly sanctioned for Ferozepore L [Very authority]	
4.8.16			Chalk & slag now obtainable for horse standings. Vegetables reduced by Base – 3 oz potatoes & 3 oz onions only by rail. Balance locally purchased. At ABBEVILLE Indians on receiving rations from us state they get them from Rail.	
5.8.16			Lucknow Bde moving to new area on 9th. No vegetables in hand now – all at dump issued. Lt Farrell's applicⁿ for R.F.C. refused.	
6.8.16			Mhow Bde relief by lorries. Petrol considered carefully but judged best to use lorries. Road maps returned to G.S. pending fresh issue. Asked DDS&T to let us have 2000 lbs [illegible] from Base for E. Rations. Units carry 3 days now. T.L.'s att to D.T. from 9th. Double issue of Rations on 7th to make lorries available.	
7.8.16			Br Tr vegetables alone come by rail – too little – informed DDS&T that Indian strength require 4 oz p.m. p.d. O/C ASC 46th & 56th Divs. BSO's to given copies of detailed orders. Double ration issue. L Bde now do not join 7th C. Mhow Bde relief.	
8.8.16			D T now carts [illegible] cards from Railhead. Sgt Duffy [illegible] moved to S Bde from S C & A. Visited Railhead.	

2353 Wt. W2544/1454 700,000 5/15 D. D. & L. A.D.S.S./Forms/C. 2118.

Instructions regarding War Diaries and Intelligence Summaries are contained in F. S. Regs., Part II. and the Staff Manual respectively. Title pages will be prepared in manuscript.

WAR DIARY
or
INTELLIGENCE SUMMARY.

(*Erase heading not required.*)

Army Form C. 2118.

Place	Date	Hour	Summary of Events and Information	Remarks and references to Appendices
8.8.16			(Cont) DDS+T re [illegible] loss of 115 lbs vegetables short received refers Borders to take over at W B weights. M[illegible] Bde horses move. R[illegible] to be fixed by Bde for lorries.	
9.8.16			Five orders of mule examined. – 17 lorries transferred to [illegible] 56th Div. Part of L Bde vanished towards St Pol without notice. Major Raymond arrives + takes over DSC from Maj Blunt. L Bde moved to new area "PAS". –	
10.8.16.			J. L. moved Horse lines. S Bde to draw on G.S. Wagons from Rhd alt: days. Visited D.D.S.+T. (Orders) Vauxhall to be transferred to [illegible] L Bde. No ASC to get act rank exceeding W.E. SSO resumed duties – visited Railhead.	
11.8.16			S. Bde to draw every 4th day on G.S.W. – distance too far. 50 men per Regt arrived. E. Rations 400 lbs biscuits. 15 lbs [illegible] 90 gur short – made up from the dump.	
12.8.16.			Visited of CRHA re rations &c. L Bde now reunited. M Bde reliant on lorries – same decision recommended. St Cooke from Sch of [illegible] ST OMER – to DAP. 2/Lt Clarke ditto to DSC.	
13.8.16			Routine. –	
14.8.16			2nd D[illegible] negative idea of exchange of agents re. Pity as this is a weak point in Bdes – They appear to have considered HSK in C. & A. esp: these are satisfactory. The point is – can any agent keep up with a Cav Regt & form the detailed link in the S[illegible] service to ensure delivery – there is no other link + this is a weak [illegible] [illegible] 2/Lt [illegible] from [illegible] to [illegible] [illegible] from HTB [illegible] to AHT [illegible] [illegible] to W.O.	
15.8.16			[illegible] 2/Lt [illegible] to [illegible] 2/Lt [illegible] [illegible] at Railhead – [illegible] the [illegible] of [illegible] [illegible] 2/Lt [illegible] to [illegible] [illegible] [illegible]	
16.8.16			Visited D.D.S.T. re [illegible] [illegible] [illegible] The important factor in [illegible] – [illegible] carcases in a [illegible] [illegible] [illegible] sound. –	
17.8.16			DAP inspected – a [illegible] unit. Lt Pearce from 3rd Army S.C. to DSC arrived.	
18.8.16			Routine	
19.8.16			Visited DSC re [illegible] – [illegible] [illegible] [illegible] [illegible] [illegible] [illegible] [illegible] [illegible] objectors as against [illegible] [illegible] [illegible] [illegible] [illegible] for 24 [illegible]	

Instructions regarding War Diaries and Intelligence Summaries are contained in F. S. Regs., Part II. and the Staff Manual respectively. Title pages will be prepared in manuscript.

WAR DIARY
or
INTELLIGENCE SUMMARY.
(Erase heading not required.)

Army Form C. 2118.

Place	Date	Hour	Summary of Events and Information	Remarks and references to Appendices
20.8.16			Routine –	
21.8.16			Visited DDS&T – I can get no real idea of how to distribute officers as the previous intimation that all STC were going seems doubtful – This point is an irksome one because the alternatives possible involve very different allocations of men to duties.	
22.8.16			Lorries for embussing [illegible] How –	
23.8.16			Lieut [?] Mackenzie suitable for Tr only – can not do Reqn or accounts – This is an example of the normal narrowness of abilities of the Temporary Officer – he is usually good at one detail only – I note this experience as it is decidedly a matter to weigh in arranging Res: of Officers later on.	
24.8.16			S/Sgt Gordon STC to arrive from Base. Pack at Base now 6oz potatoes 2oz vegetables full strength.	
25.8.16			Routine	
26.8.16			S.Sgt Gordon arrived	
27.8.16			1lb potatoes = 2 lbs fr vegetables – we have rather underdrawn these as two S&Ts thought the equivalents were equal weights. There are a number of such cases wh: recur + the scales are difficult to follow as they are altered piecemeal + rarely republished up to date.	
28.8.16			Routine Met O/C ASC 2nd [?] Dn at ABBEVILLE after long runs. 2nd Dn differs from us in various details due to understood factors.	
29.8.16			Emphatic DDS&T circular re BSS, 3316, 3317 – our accounts described as very much the best in Third Army: as they should be for this circular is not on our account – but I got a D/O published to keep up attention to the points involved.	
30.8.16			DDS&T calls on us to take delivery of a lot of coal for other Dns – DHQ gave us working parties at once + all will be well.	
31.8.16				

[signature] Lt Col
O/C ASC [illegible] Dn

2353 Wt. W2544/1454 700,000 5/15 D. D. & L. A.D.S.S./Forms/C. 2118.

1916 JAN – 1916 SEP

WAR DIARY
or
INTELLIGENCE SUMMARY.

(Erase heading not required.)

Army Form C. 2118.

Instructions regarding War Diaries and Intelligence Summaries are contained in F. S. Regs., Part II. and the Staff Manual respectively. Title pages will be prepared in manuscript.

Place	Date	Hour	Summary of Events and Information	Remarks and references to Appendices
1.9.16			Orders for 3rd received – notice [illegible]	
2.9.16			Routine + arrangements for move as usual	
3.9.16			The move involves today's concentration of 3 Bdes under 3 Corps orders and [illegible] the 1st [illegible] again [illegible] them. One of these Bdes comes under our S/T as regards [illegible] + [illegible] from another Dn – rest continued to be supplied by us. At the same time we start 2 days [illegible] lifting 1 Bde + 1 Regt DMs + 10 Regt DM's kits + R.T'd [illegible] our own M H T [illegible] according to a Tr map modified by having the large [illegible] + all S of one important road placed out of bounds. We also have [illegible] but feed 2 Batteries + [illegible] D A C + DAP + provide the 3rd Coy with 3rd Rations	
4.9.16			Moved as above – 1 Regt did not get DM's kits for night of 4/5th – all rest smoothly done.	
5.9.16			DM's concentrated with kits complete – The usual trouble with O/C DM who has read the standing instructions that could before has not got his copy, has done nothing and [illegible] states he decided not to take an interest! There is no way I can think of to ensure organised mechanical working but to allocate a trained S/T N.C.O. to each unit with an understudy – It is absolutely necessary to do this + it is patent in the field that no matter what arguments are used to prove + establish the theory that Regtl men will comply with S/T systems the solid fact remains that they don't + won't + prefer to stand + curse the 'intricacies' of a B.S.S. etc + take such censures as eventuate rather than learn anything about S + T. – I see this over + over again – it is a matter of course in every formation and there are times when the unit needs [illegible] of a unit is not [illegible] by the S/O. I am convinced that a member of the S Service should be with each unit with an understudy to serve detachments but under BSO's control	
6.9.16			Routine	
			Orders for move on 9th issued + in evening [illegible] as doubtful	
7.9.16			cancelled. DM's to move on 9th [illegible] from [illegible] destination. A H T Coy moving to A H T D [illegible]. Orders for move on 9th [illegible] Park is moving to TALMAS + comes under 4th Army – DM's leave tomorrow + are fed	
8.9.16			get 8 S wagons [illegible] about 11th [illegible] by 4th A. near ALBERT. – We presumably [illegible] later on.	
9.9.16			Traffic [illegible] map borrowed from [illegible] returned to Q – DDS+T replied to [illegible] dump to R.S.O.'s charge. SS [illegible] Railhead to be carried forward by 2 days Corps Echelons. We have asked DDS+T to increase vegetable pack – Thus Reqd Officers will not need cars.	

S.S. 2353 Wt. W2544/1454 700,000 5/15 D. D. & L. A.D.S.S./Forms/C. 2118.

Army Form C. 2118.

Instructions regarding War Diaries and Intelligence Summaries are contained in F. S. Regs., Part II. and the Staff Manual respectively. Title pages will be prepared in manuscript.

WAR DIARY
or
INTELLIGENCE SUMMARY.

(Erase heading not required.)

Place	Date	Hour	Summary of Events and Information	Remarks and references to Appendices
10.9.16			Routine –	
11.9.16			Moved to DOULLENS – With AA+QMG visited Cav Corps H.Q. – ADS+T's office interviewed & took down some details regarding new Lucknow Train & Scale of rations – Recd L Bde complaints. L S Train Ration scale seems to me largely unsuitable but it was fixed by advice of Ind Dn & no modification is to be considered. The L Bde complaints [illegible] to be hearsay of [illegible] taken up [illegible] by the normal authority [illegible] very vague ideas on food!	
12.9.16			Referred to AA+QMG orders regarding Special Scale of Rations for Lucknow Train, Replied to Lucknow Bde Complaints. Nothing can be done about the ration scale but I am going to replace at least half the Atta by biscuits for Indians will not be able to cook when there are [illegible] — This important mistake arises solely from there being no one on the Admin line who knows Indians rations – nor is there extant any set of ration scales suitable for varied circumstances available for Admin authorities – To compile such a book would be a useful measure as every set of operations involve various forces & 'imaginary scales' are suggested even by sowars here & they come direct to [illegible] almost unconsidered – Every unit wants something different & often articles they would not like if they got them. A set of scales on which not only issues but reserves on L of C might be calculated would be useful.	
13.9.16			Moved to Querrieu & Allonville – Rly to be FRECHENCOURT. – DSC carries RSO, Estab & Ind Ration Reserves. Moved to Querrieu. Orders to move on 15th – O/C ASC Commands A Echelon of Dn. Issued orders to Bdes & D.T. & Ambulances.	
14.9.16				
15.9.16			Moved off at 5 am. Checked at CORBIE level xing & convoy cut 5 times at this point – It was 3 miles long. Parked at forking of the track to Ville sur Ancre and convoy started complete after M'tow Bde had gone thro – At a check 1 mile further on passing the route of gaps thro the trench system Lucknow Bde cut us twice diagonally & again W of the Bivouac, filed into Bivouac – no casualties – av. pace 3 miles per hour.	
16.9.16			Routine – Mistake not to have a clerk as had been desired – Its one too much to pen & paper.	
17.9.16			B Ech is drawing from Frechencourt for Br & Animals but we send Indians rations back. Railhead now Albert – Slightly shelled at intervals but virtually no casualties & the Rly Stn & garages never hit I think	

2353 Wt. W2544/1454 700,000 5/15 D. D. & L. A.D.S.S./Forms/C. 2118.

Instructions regarding War Diaries and Intelligence Summaries are contained in F. S. Regs., Part II. and the Staff Manual respectively. Title pages will be prepared in manuscript.

WAR DIARY
or
INTELLIGENCE SUMMARY.
(*Erase heading not required.*)

Army Form C. 2118.

Place	Date	Hour	Summary of Events and Information	Remarks and references to Appendices
			The train arrival times are irregular (& of course result in movement irregularity) & this to some extent affects loading labour – which has to stand ready for hours & load hurriedly. This a strain. We now load in bulk & divide amongst the lorries afterwards	
18.9.16.			Routine – Rain [illegible] – Train loaded lorries at 5 am 19th	
19.9.16			Routine. Ordered – Extra 1 days [illegible] to be carried on DSC – Today's [illegible] 20th	
20.9.16			Hay [illegible] 5 lbs per animal – Balance 5 lbs drawn from CARBIE Barges.	
21.9.16			[illegible] 1 days for consumption & 1 day to be carried on A.S.C. wagons – replenished from CARBIE [illegible] E.F.	
22.9.16			[illegible] to be rationed by us – 10 lbs of hay [illegible] per animal.	
23.9.16			[illegible] 5 lbs per [illegible] of hay to be loaded separately on DSC in case of an early move. Potatoes reduced to 3 oz. Train arrived 5 pm.	
			The second [illegible] to FRICOURT [illegible] Bde near QUERRIEU [illegible]. In the evening returned to [illegible]	
25.9.16			Routine – The 19th [illegible] D.S. [illegible] after their fight – we had 2 lorries exactly loaded with 1 days rations each to [illegible]	
26.9.16				
27.9.16			Returned back to BUSSY area & [illegible] – L.G.S. Wagon lorries [illegible] to CARBIE barges [illegible] to DSC & [illegible] – latter had just been [illegible] no available lorries to lift these supplies & the L.G.S. train had to go to No 16 Rail Park. [illegible] on checking lists.	

Instructions regarding War Diaries and Intelligence Summaries are contained in F. S. Regs., Part II. and the Staff Manual respectively. Title pages will be prepared in manuscript.

WAR DIARY
or
INTELLIGENCE SUMMARY.
(Erase heading not required.)

Army Form C. 2118.

Place	Date	Hour	Summary of Events and Information	Remarks and references to Appendices
28.9.16			Railhead CORBIE, DDS&T Fourth Army asks to reduce 60% meat & 75% bread. Lt Lupton moved to area in advance, for move to PICQUIGNY area — Jodhpore Lancers "blew out" to FREVENT(?) without orders — this "unit" is a peculiar one — it is not budgetted for or settled in strength — it is an a body of men & horses which is fed on Br rations but with Indian meat on Br scale — except when it adds to its strength by sudden absorptions from the J. Lancers. It has no Transport & varies from a few men to 45 men & 30 horses. It is like nothing else in France & is a long perpetual worry & anxiety — It blows in & out of the Dn apparently with the breezes & is a "political" factor & has to be watched & considered as such. It has no organisation, never complains or asks [illegible] the form of rations one never knows the facts if all is really well with it. Returned L. S. Train to 10th Res Park.	
29.9.16			Dn moved to BILLY LE HAUT CLOCHER area, Rhd St Riquier — Lt Lupton sent on to reconnoitre new area for potatoes vegetables & wood. Cav Corps H.Q. overlaps Fourth Army H.Q. & G.H.Q. functions here as in other ways & did not apparently move the D.S.C. [illegible]	
30.9.16			Railhead BEAURAINVILLE — Dn moved to CRECY area — Visited D.D.S.&T. G.H.Q. — got all the limits he could & was understood at once & every facility re fuel, vegetable prices &c ready & given. [illegible]	

[illegible] Lt Col
O/C A.S.C. 1st [illegible] Dn

2353 Wt. W2544/1454 700,000 5/15 D. D. & L. A.D.S.S./Forms/C. 2118.

B.E.F. FRANCE & FLANDERS.

1 INDIAN CAVALRY DIVISION.

H.Q. GENERAL STAFF.

COMMANDER ROYAL ENGINEERS.

1914 AUG TO 1915 FEB.

DEPUTY ASSISTANT DIRECTOR ORDNANCE SERVICES.

1914 AUG TO 1916 DEC

ASST DIR VETERINARY SERVICES

1916 JULY TO 1916 DEC.

ASST DIR SUPPLY & TRANSPORT

1914 SEPT TO 1916 SEPT.

1169

B.E.F. FRANCE & FLANDERS

1 INDIAN CAVALRY DIV

H.Q. GENERAL STAFF.

COMMANDER ROYAL ENGINEE

1914 AUG TO 1915 FEB.

DEPUTY ASSISTANT DIR ORDNANCE SERVICES.

1914 AUG TO 1916 DEC

ASST DIR VETERINARY SERVICES

1916 JULY TO 1916 DEC.

ASST DIR SUPPLY & TRANS

1914 SEPT TO 1916 SEPT

www.ingramcontent.com/pod-product-compliance
Lightning Source LLC
Chambersburg PA
CBHW081532160426
43191CB00011B/1744

* 9 7 8 1 4 7 4 5 0 1 4 0 8 *